T0361026

ROUTLEDGE LIBRARY EDITIONS:
RETAILING AND DISTRIBUTION

RETAILING AND THE PUBLIC

RETAILING AND THE PUBLIC

LAWRENCE E. NEAL

Volume 8

Routledge
Taylor & Francis Group

LONDON AND NEW YORK

First published in 1932

This edition first published in 2013
by Routledge
2 Park Square, Milton Park, Abingdon, Oxon, OX14 4RN

Simultaneously published in the USA and Canada
by Routledge
711 Third Avenue, New York, NY 10017

Routledge is an imprint of the Taylor & Francis Group, an informa business

© George Allen & Unwin Ltd, 1932

All rights reserved. No part of this book may be reprinted or reproduced or utilised in any form or by any electronic, mechanical, or other means, now known or hereafter invented, including photocopying and recording, or in any information storage or retrieval system, without permission in writing from the publishers.

Trademark notice: Product or corporate names may be trademarks or registered trademarks, and are used only for identification and explanation without intent to infringe.

British Library Cataloguing in Publication Data
A catalogue record for this book is available from the British Library

ISBN: 978-0-415-51032-5 (Set)
eISBN: 978-0-203-10362-3 (Set)
ISBN: 978-0-415-62414-5 (Volume 8)
eISBN: 978-0-203-10368-5 (Volume 8)

Publisher's Note
The publisher has gone to great lengths to ensure the quality of this reprint but points out that some imperfections in the original copies may be apparent.

Disclaimer
The publisher has made every effort to trace copyright holders and would welcome correspondence from those they have been unable to trace.

MIX
Paper from
responsible sources
FSC
www.fsc.org   FSC® C013604

Printed and bound by CPI Group (UK) Ltd, Croydon, CR0 4YY

RETAILING AND THE PUBLIC

BY

LAWRENCE E. NEAL

Joint Managing Director of Daniel Neal & Sons Ltd

WITH A FOREWORD BY

F. J. MARQUIS, M.A., B.Sc., J.P.

President, Incorporated Association of Retail Distributors ;
Joint Managing Director, Lewis's Ltd, Liverpool
Manchester, Birmingham, Leeds and Glasgow

LONDON
GEORGE ALLEN & UNWIN LTD
MUSEUM STREET

FIRST PUBLISHED 1932

All rights reserved

PRINTED IN GREAT BRITAIN BY THE ABERDEEN UNIVERSITY PRESS LTD

CONTENTS

PAGE

FOREWORD, BY F. J. MARQUIS, M.A., B.SC., J.P. . . . vii

INTRODUCTION xiii

PART I

SECTION 1

SURVEY OF RETAILING ORGANISATIONS

CHAPTER

   I. PRELIMINARY 1

  II. THE SMALL INDEPENDENT SHOP 5

 III. THE SPECIALITY SHOP 10

 IV. THE DEPARTMENTAL STORE 14

  V. THE MULTIPLE SHOP 27

 VI. THE CO-OPERATIVE MOVEMENT 39

VII. THE "FIXED-PRICE" CHAIN STORE 48

VIII. THE CHARACTERISTICS OF MULTIPLE ORGANISATIONS . 54

 IX. CLUB TRADING 59

  X. MAIL ORDER BUSINESS 62

SECTION 2

THE DEPARTMENTAL STORE IN ACTION

  XI. THE BUILDING 66

 XII. THE ORGANISATION 79

XIII. BUDGETARY CONTROL OF MERCHANDISING . . . 89

XIV. BUDGETARY CONTROL OF EXPENSES 103

PART II

TO-DAY AND TO-MORROW

 XV. AN OBJECTIVE ANALYSIS OF RETAILING . . . 127

XVI. FUTURE TRENDS 150

FOREWORD

By F. J. Marquis, M.A., B.Sc., J.P.

President, Incorporated Association of Retail Distributors ;
Joint Managing Director, Lewis's Ltd, Liverpool,
Manchester, Birmingham, Leeds and Glasgow

THIS book is significant. It arises from the new generation.
Whilst the desire to teach is inherent in the mind of
man, it is not usual for those who teach to be also people
who " do." The weakness of much of the economic
writing that has been poured forth during all the commercial and industrial disturbances of the last twenty
years arises from the fact that it has come from the pens of
men who have had little of the devastating experience of
practical business. The discussions that gave rise to this
book took place among young men whom the schools and
universities of this country have had a hand in moulding :
but they have been through the further process of education which comes from occupying positions of control in
business life. With minds trained in the processes of
accurate thought, they have looked on the world of business
and found it sadly confusing—and from the confusion they
have seen economic waste springing up, as indeed it does
all over the place. That clear sight is one of their assets :
another is their comparative youth. They are young
enough to see visions of orderliness and reasonableness
in human relations : they have faith enough to dare to
paint some outline at least of a picture of reconstruction.
They have fashioned their hope of the future through the
furnace of hard discussion. One night they were kind

enough to invite me to attend one of their meetings under the disguise that I might help them. I left in a state of wonderment. They seemed to me to have abandoned all allegiance to the political ideas of the past and to have a new world in view. It was vastly encouraging to find men who might have looked forward with some contentment to harvesting profits from businesses which older generations had founded—and founded well—recognising that this post-war period was demanding of them something more courageous than the traversing of well-marked roads.

I urge this book and its motives on the attention of those inclined to pessimism regarding the future. The industrial life of England is safe in the hands of a generation that dares to question its inheritance and has the enterprise to seek, in this severely practical way, to survey and then to rebuild British Commerce. And the subject they have chosen is auspicious. They have resisted the temptation to survey and rebuild the policy of the Bank of England or the large-scale industries of this country : they have come to earth and dealt with shop-keeping. A generation ago such a subject would have been too small for such intelligence, and yet it is a trade of major importance. No other industry so closely touches the common life of the people. It gives direct employment to more people than any other single trade. Over one-half of the national income is concerned with it. The gigantic figure of £1,750,000,000 passed through it in the year 1930, during which time the attention of politicians was riveted on the Imports and Exports of the country which totalled respectively £1,040,000,000 and £570,000,000.

No other industry so widely affects the public as does this work of retailing, and in none other is there such a wide range of scale. In half a million shops men and women are struggling to earn a living by meeting and anticipating public wants. They are collectively determining the prices people pay for the necessities of life. They represent the public : in the long run they are the masters of the manufacturers and producers : they give the orders for goods : they are the final court of judgment on the artistic and utilitarian capacity of each of the producers of consumable stores. And again I repeat, there are 500,000 of them. It is a disturbing thought even for the most democratic of minds to contemplate. Manufacturers certainly will welcome the motive that prompts this book, for if shop-keeping could be systematised, if the individual preferences and prejudices of the retailers could somehow be canalised, then there would be some hope of production being organised on some less wasteful and more scientific lines.

This is a problem that concerns the public and the statesman. The latter has recently been disturbed by the level of retail prices. He has, generally speaking, fallen into the error of comparing the fall that has taken place in commodity prices and in retail prices, and, with a rather unaccountable failure to realise that the labour that enters so largely in turning raw materials into finished articles of wear has not fallen by any large percentage, he has concluded that retailers were making unduly large profits. Alas, such is not the case : if it were, then preventive machinery, such as the Consumers' Council, could be effective. The truth is that the gap in

prices, such as it is, brings profit to no one. The public
is largely responsible, and that through thoughtlessness
and ignorance of the facts. This book may help to bring
enlightenment. It makes clear to those who will read
it how widespread are the services that are involved in
retailing. The complexity of the organisation of a large
department store—in which the authors are obviously
much more widely experienced than in the more elementary form of distributing—is a source of wide public
interest.

But when the public stops to consider the cost of the
services it buys, it may well be alarmed. These everyday facts of " terms of credit," of the services of transport
organisations for carrying goods home, of the immense
varieties of colour and styles which all shops are expected
to stock, of the great variety in prices designed to meet
every sort of pocket : these are factors in retailing which
under the forces of competition are growing rapidly,
and in the opinion of some of us are making the cost
of distribution much too high. It may reasonably be
questioned whether, if the public recognised the cost
of these " services," they would not, in their wisdom,
decide to have less of them and exchange them for
lower prices. The retailer's proper function is to concentrate public demand on the smallest range of colours,
styles, sizes, etc., that will give the public the best value
from the manufacturing organisations that make these
things. To do this work he needs the understanding
support of those whom he serves. It may also be that
the reading of this book will make intelligent people of
all classes wonder whether the free play of unrestricted

competition is a national asset. I approach the subject without political consideration—but if, as I believe, the economic salvation of this country is coming along the lines of scientific planning of commercial services, then there is something to make us think in the statement the author makes that there is now one shop to every twenty houses in urban areas.

I am not sure what sort of public this book will reach. Obviously those engaged in large-scale distributing will welcome it, and find stimulus from the depth of its thoughtfulness. But I wish the public would read it, and particularly I wish that women would consider the questions it raises. For women are the great dictators of the distributing trade : they hold its future in control— and they can do such a vast amount to help it and to help the economy of the family budget. Shopping is a necessity to most people, but to women—I think to most women—it represents a great pleasure. It may be that the reading of this book will persuade them to begin the era of national economic planning. To take the smallest example, if they would decide to plan their shopping hours, the cost of retailing could be quite appreciably reduced. If those who could shop in the morning would do so : if the peaks and the valleys of shopping could be levelled somewhat, the large army of shop assistants would lead much happier lives, the services the public received would be much more efficient—and the cost of it could be reduced. The intelligent use of spending power would be infinitely more effective than restrictive legislation in bringing down cost.

This problem of retailing has never been recognised as

the vital factor that it is in national life. The standard of living of the mass of the people depends upon it. If it is carried on as a national service, it consciously seeks to give the best for the lowest price : it strives to bring all the luxuries of beauty in design and taste within the reach of the maximum number of people. By concentration of demand it enables manufacturers to produce cheaply—and in the volume of the production to ignore the cost of improvements in style, cut or colouring.

By such means it has been possible to effect the change, that can justly be described as a revolution, in the standard of dress and of home comforts of the working classes. This has been the sociological justification of the large-scale retailer during this generation. The work is not finished. To-day we are apt to wonder whether the general standard of living has become too high. How can it be too high ? Surely the desire to possess beautiful homes and pleasant-looking clothes is a great national asset : it is a stimulus to effort—and since the forces of production for the moment have outstepped the effective demand for them, it is wise of us to give some further consideration to our home trade, and particularly to the aspect of it with which this book deals in a manner at once scientific in its analysis and stimulating in its constructive vision.

INTRODUCTION

IT is fast becoming a commonplace that the problem which confronts twentieth-century industry is the problem of distribution, but the initial difficulty is that even the general configuration of the country to be traversed is so little known. Undoubtedly retailing occupies the largest territory, and yet it can be safely stated that even to-day there is an entire lack of an adequate chart or map for retailing. Accordingly, these pages are an attempt to effect some preliminary survey of the ground, to sketch in certain salient features, and to indicate possible lines of further approach. The work is, in fact, a direct product of discussions which have been taking place for two years past among a small group who are themselves wholly engaged in retailing. In the first instance, therefore, they were frankly concerned to take stock of their own position. Nor is it perhaps unnatural that a younger generation which has come into commerce since the war and has spent some years, during a period of changing scene and tempo, in mastering the intricacies of that section of the trade to which each individually has been attached, should feel a need in the difficult circumstances of the 1930's for getting a more general idea of their bearings.

But as the subject is already one of considerable public moment, further enquiry soon enlarged the horizon ; and the group came to feel that it might not be out of place to attempt a more ambitious contribution. Possibly, for instance, an account of this kind could do something to promote a parallel quickening of interest among other retailers in the larger issues of their function ? Could it also help to create in the minds of the outside public (including those engaged in Productive Industry) an awareness of the complexities involved and of the severely limiting factors in any readjustment of distribution to the likely needs of the immediate future ? And as the belief inevitably grew that readjustment must come, did not the very limitations and complexities in themselves constitute a definite and urgent challenge to action ?

The book falls conveniently into two parts. In the earlier part, Section 1, which has been handled somewhat separately both in its drafting and in its method of approach, contains a bird's-eye view of the general lie of the land, so as to provide a rapid survey of the recent historical growth of retailing and an assessment of its various present forms. This is followed in Section 2 by a more detailed and descriptive picture of the actual workings of a departmental store. Attention has been concentrated for the most part on the orderly marshalling of these activities ; but it is important that there should also be some appreciation of the shifting kaleidoscope and the hazards of the market-place. The rough and tumble will remain for the individual trader, however careful the foresight and however good the organisation.

Part 2 attempts a more critical and searching analysis of the whole pattern of retailing, leading up to the final chapter, which is frankly a piece of experimental forecasting.

As the work proceeded, therefore, there has been a change in the angle of approach away from the subjective view which had stimulated the initial enquiry into the workings of one's own job, and on to a consciously objective analysis of the situation ; this in turn giving place to a yet more constructive attitude and finally to an attempted new synthesis. Possibly it may not escape attention that this process has been accompanied by a mental evolution, which during the course of the enquiry has been tending to lay more and more stress on the need to consider retailing not just as a more or less haphazard agglomeration of shopkeepers—however efficient the pick of them might prove to be on an individual showing—but as fundamentally the organisation, parallel with production, of the necessary supply services for a nation's daily wants and needs.

The first plea, therefore, is that Production and Distribution should be considered as complementary halves to each other ; and the second is that we should cease to pour new wine into old bottles. Freedom for enterprise and innovation is all too difficult within the framework of an economic structure that is becoming over much of its area outdated and outworn. Indeed, the restrictive grip of such a structure can be more severe even than that of any set of regulations : for circumstance is raised on a pedestal ; and the potentialities of a whole generation are in danger of being frustrated and becoming of little account.

Both for his personal help and by reason of his wealth of experience a very great debt is owed to Mr. F. Chitham, the Chairman of the Incorporated Association of Retail Distributors. His friendly challenge at the start set us on the road : while his practical advice and guidance thereafter have been a source of very real encouragement in a work that has admittedly been arduous because it has had to be carried on solely in spare time. This last point may perhaps be legitimately advanced to excuse some of its known shortcomings.

To the Secretary of the same body, Mr. E. J. B. Lloyd, who has been constantly in attendance, no less thanks are due. As a friendly critic throughout his contribution is naturally a very large and distinctive one.

The group itself has been drawn from those actively and responsibly engaged in retailing both in London and the provinces. It comprises Mr. R. G. Alexander, Mr. F. R. Barker, Mr. D. Catesby, Mr. R. Cohen, Mr. C. W. Denham, Mr. D. B. Morgan. Their unfailing helpfulness has made the task of chairmanship a very real pleasure ; and the absence of any further acknowledgments to them individually should therefore only serve to emphasise that this work is a joint effort, and that any significance which it may possess is derived from the co-operative spirit which has animated it.

LAWRENCE E. NEAL

PART I

Section 1. Survey of Retailing Organisations

CHAPTER I

PRELIMINARY SURVEY

BEFORE attempting any critical examination of the way in which retail distribution in this country to-day is performing its economic function in providing a link between the producer and consumer, it is important to get a clear idea of the existing structure. Although the essential function remains the same, different types of distributive organisation have in course of time been developed within that framework, and these attack the problem in various ways. Each has a peculiar technique of its own, and it is well that the object which each is striving to attain should be clearly grasped ; for criticisms which may properly be directed against one do not necessarily apply to the rest, and while it may be thought that retail distribution as a whole is in some respects wasteful and extravagant, there will be found within its compass one or more different types of organisation which are undoubtedly doing an excellent job.

In trying to determine how these various types have developed, the historical approach gives very little help. Up to the middle of the nineteenth century the history of retail distribution provides few landmarks. Daniel Defoe's " Compleat English Tradesman," which appeared in 1725, gives a picture of retailing in this country at that time which probably remained true for another hundred years at least. During the whole of this period the typical distributive unit was undoubtedly the small shop, but the proprietor of it was something more than a mere distributor of merchandise. He was essentially a specialist in the goods which he handled, and was in many cases something of a craftsman as well. He depended a great deal on the personal connections which he was able to build up in his immediate neighbourhood, and hence, no doubt, the common expression of " family butcher " or " family baker."

In spite of the Industrial Revolution towards the end of the eighteenth century and the enormous development of transport facilities which followed in the first half of the nineteenth century, it was not until the 1850's that there was any perceptible tendency in distribution towards large-scale business parallel with what was taking place in other spheres of industry and commerce. In 1852, however, the Bon Marché, which has the reputation of being the first departmental store, was established in Paris, and before 1860 there were examples of this type of store in the U.S.A., where the Great Atlantic and Pacific Tea Company, which is a multiple branch organisation and now the largest retail concern in the world, had also been founded by that date. In this country Whiteley's appeared soon after 1860, and about the same time Sir Thomas Lipton laid the foundations of the firm which still bears his name. During the next two generations, and particularly since the beginning of the present century, large-scale retailing has made great strides, and although the growth has been curiously haphazard, it is possible to isolate two main lines of development from the small distributive unit of Defoe's time : (1) either the field of merchandise was extended so as in effect to bring a number of single shops under one roof, thus paving the way for the departmental store, or (2) both distributive unit and merchandise were standardised and the field of operations extended over a series of shopping districts, thus giving birth to the multiple shop organisation.

The urge towards large-scale distribution came unquestionably from the paramount necessity of finding economic channels through which the vastly increased output of production could find its way to the consumer. The forms taken by these various types of organisation, which now go to make up the patchwork of retail distribution as it exists to-day, were probably governed by the over-riding factor that it takes all sorts to make a world, and different kinds of retail service were created to satisfy the varying needs that arose. The first section of this book has therefore been devoted to a critical survey of the more distinctive kinds of retail organisation that at present exist, and of the peculiar technique which they have each developed, to meet the special demand for which they are catering.

There is first the Small Independent Shop, and coupled with it the Speciality Shop, which may be regarded either as a development from the small independent shop, or as possibly the direct successor of the old craftsman-retailer to whom reference has been made. Secondly, there is the Departmental Store, which has made a very considerable contribution to modern retailing, and has probably been responsible to a larger degree than any other type for altering the whole outlook of the public towards shopping. Thirdly, there is the Multiple Branch Organisation, which seems the one best adapted for providing mass distribution as the counterpart of mass production, and in the succeeding chapters has been handled under three different aspects. There is the Multiple Shop organisation proper, which concentrates on a single field of merchandise and has been made familiar by the multiple grocers, butchers, and many others ; secondly, the Co-Operative Movement, with all its many ramifications ; and the third and youngest, but by no means the least virile variation, namely, the Fixed Price Chain Store, like Woolworth's.

Finally, there are certain cross-currents in retailing which should not be overlooked in a survey of this description. There is first the Mail Order business, which, owing to the rapid growth of road transport, seems to be a declining factor, both in this country and in other parts of the world. There is also the Club system of trading, which in certain parts of England and Wales has become such an integral part of retail distribution that it cannot be ignored. It now remains to examine in greater detail the technique which these different kinds of distributive organisation adopt, the objects which they set out to achieve, and the functions which they severally perform.

CHAPTER II

THE SMALL INDEPENDENT SHOP

NUMERICALLY, and in virtue of his aggregate turnover, the small independent retailer is still by far the most important of the various channels of distribution. It has been estimated with some authority that there are about 500,000 retail shops in the country. Of these, probably not more than 10 per cent. belong to the various chain stores and multiple branch organisations, including co-operative societies, so that upwards of 90 per cent. are of the small independent type. In the absence of reliable statistics, it is impossible to place any accurate figure on the proportion of the total retail trade of the country for which in the aggregate these outlets are responsible, but probably between 50 and 60 per cent. is not far off the mark. This means that of the existing retail outlets the 10 per cent. which belong to the multiple companies and other forms of large-scale retailing account for possibly 45 per cent. or more of the trade.

This multiplicity of retail shops is one of the problems with which distribution is faced to-day, and it may assist in getting the whole picture in proper perspective if some attempt is made to determine the character, apart from the number, of these small independent shops. The available sources of information about this subject are not very numerous, but considerable light is thrown on it by the results of an investigation conducted by the Home Office and Ministry of Labour in 1930 (" Report of Select Committee on Shop Assistants," vol. 2). In the course of their report it is stated that in Birmingham, with a population of 950,000, there are some 21,000 retail shops, of which no less than 75 per cent. are of the family type, i.e. employing no assistants except members of the family. In Leeds, with a population of about 500,000, there are some 9700 shops, of which 7300, or just over 75 per cent., are of this type. It has been ascertained from another source that in Sheffield, out of a total of 11,743 retail shops, 9082, or over 77 per cent., belong to the same class. What is even more significant is that among the shops that have been established during the last ten years to meet the requirements of new housing schemes in Birmingham, the number of family shops is still as high as 65 per cent.

If these figures can be taken as typical, and there is other evidence to suggest that they are, it may reasonably be assumed that certainly more than half, and possibly as much as two-thirds, of the existing retail shops are of the family type. In other words, they have probably been established, not with any conscious object of providing the distributive link between the producer and the consumer, but in order to use the proceeds, if any, to help in paying the rent of the dwelling-house, or to eke out other sources of income. Indeed, the whole tendency of recent productive development, of which the tobacco and confectionery trades are possibly the clearest example, has been to make it easy for a person with little capital, and less business training or commercial experience, to open a retail shop. This tendency has apparently been strong enough to enable the number of small shops to increase side by side with a remarkable development

during the last twenty-five years in large-scale distribution, which, in so far as it is not accounted for by an expansion in the national income during the same period,
must have been at the expense of the small retailer.

Now, in the sense that it fosters the spirit of indepen-
dence, it might possibly be argued that it is desirable from
the social point of view to encourage the small shop, but
it must not be forgotten that the haphazard, uncontrolled
proliferation of these units gives rise to economic difficulties both for the retailer himself and for the commercial
community generally. These difficulties are largely due
to the inadequate turnover which the small shop can expect
to achieve. While, again, no figures are available for this
country, a census of distribution carried out in 1926 in
respect of eleven cities in the United States showed that of
all the then existing retail outlets 75 per cent. had an annual
turnover of less than the equivalent of £10,000 each, with
an average of less than £2000 per annum. Allowing for the
higher level of American prices and for the fall in retail
prices which has taken place since 1926, it is probable
that the average annual turnover of the small shop in this
country to-day is, if anything, less than £2000. This
means that on such a turnover the small retailer, if he is
to survive at all, cannot reduce the gross margin between
the price he charges to his customer and the price he pays
to his supplier, and it is of course this margin which
represents to the consumer the cost of retail distribution.
It also means that with his small purchasing power he
cannot buy on such favourable terms as his larger competitors, and for his merchandise he has generally to rely
on what is offered to him by wholesalers, to whom he may

already be tied by financial obligations, instead of being able to create a demand by aggressive advertising for his own lines, or, like some of the large distributive organisations, to control production from the raw material upwards.

Again, the small retailer is frequently handicapped by his ignorance of modern technique in the conduct of his business, so that neither by close supervision of his stock to ensure economical use of the capital employed, nor by watchful control of his expenses can he keep an active grip on his affairs. The result is that money is often being lost without his being aware of it.

At the same time, although too often small-scale retailing is rashly embarked upon as an easy means of livelihood, it should not be forgotten that in the personal contact which he is able to maintain with his customers the efficient small shopkeeper has an immense advantage over his larger competitors. Where he sets out to exploit that personal contact, and to satisfy the small everyday needs of a carefully selected class of customer in his own neighbourhood, there is no doubt that he performs a definite and useful function, even though at a higher cost than some of his better organised competitors.

There are still several fields of retailing which do not appear to lend themselves to large-scale organisation, and here it is safe to say that the small unit will always flourish. Moreover, signs are not lacking, both in this country and in America, that the force of competition from multiple organisations and departmental stores is compelling the small retailer to put his own house in order and to do a more efficient job. He is not only learning some of the technique which the multiples have taught him, but, particularly in the United States and Canada, is beginning to form himself into voluntary associations for the purpose of securing the advantages of bulk buying. Moreover, these associations are paying increasing attention to the selling side as well, and insist, as a condition of membership, that their members should modernise shop-fronts and fixtures and improve their selling service. This latter movement has so far made little progress in this country, although certain co-operative buying organisations already exist, especially in the grocery trade. It is something, however, that a beginning has been made, and certainly in America it has been suggested with some conviction that one of the causes of the check to chain store expansion has been the improved service offered by the independent retailer.

CHAPTER III

THE SPECIALITY SHOP

THE Speciality Shop almost certainly owes its origin to the craftsman who was a recognised authority on the merchandise—be it books, footwear or fishing tackle—in which he dealt. That type of shop still exists in a great number of different trades, and must clearly be distinguished from the ordinary retail unit discussed in the last section. Its success depends on the first-hand knowledge and personality of the proprietor, and other characteristics of enthusiasm and initiative which will always enable it to out-distance less intelligent competition. Such an establishment would now be described as a " Speciality Shop," but although that term is falling into common usage it is a comparatively recent importation, and is difficult to define with any precision, because it is applied to so many apparently different types of organisation. Not only do those types seem to differ from one another, but even within each type there are a great many gradations both in size and in the class of trade done, so that it becomes a little misleading to include them all under one heading. In the last resort, however, they all have this one feature in common that, in some form or another, they represent an expression of specialised knowledge brought to bear on a comparatively restricted range of merchandise. Within that range each seeks to do a better and more individual job than its rivals in the retailing field.

It is perhaps natural that the modern speciality shop is most frequently met with in the women's wear trade, but taking even a small section of this one trade there are a great many variations to be found. At the one end there is the small exclusive shop which is a specialist within the restricted field it has selected. It may concentrate, for example, on model gowns or millinery, in which fashion is the all-important element, and depend for its custom not so much on keenly cut prices or the wide range of merchandise that it offers within this field as on the individuality, novelty and good taste of its stock. It relies for its prosperity on its successful interpretation of fashion, on a careful selection of the merchandise itself, and particularly on the personal and intimate connection between proprietor and clientele. Moreover, the individuality of this kind of speciality shop expresses itself not only in the merchandise it sells and the way in which it is displayed, but also in the premises it occupies ; and those premises must generally be located in certain recognised shopping centres in which rent and rates are high, and where such shops tend to congregate. Again, its fixtures and fittings have to be carefully selected with the same end in view ; while the type of assistant it employs must be in keeping with its stock, and the somewhat discriminating clientele which it sets out to serve. Even in this type of speciality shop, however, there is plenty of room for variation in technique according to the class of trade which is aimed at. The exclusive shop in Knightsbridge, catering for a high-class clientele, will be expected to extend credit and provide other services which do not arise in the case of the Shaftesbury Avenue shop that has a different type of customer in mind. Although this difference in technique may be reflected in the prices charged, in neither case is it price alone which represents the primary appeal.

At the other end of the scale there is the large multiple organisation, such as C. & A. Modes, which handles the problem in quite a different way. While specialising in the same field of fashion merchandise, it sets out to cater for the multitude, and the price element at once becomes of primary importance. Specialised knowledge in this instance takes the form of supplying within a given range as large a variety of size, style and colour as is consistent with rapid turnover and low prices. Consequently the premises in which business is carried on are larger and have less of that distinctive personality which has just been described. The example of C. & A. Modes, which belongs to a type of distribution of comparatively recent development, is particularly interesting from another point of view, in that it illustrates the combination of mass production methods with a multiple distributive organisation. This combination, while not uncommon in other spheres, has in this instance been applied to fashion merchandise, which at first sight would appear to be a most unpromising field.

Parallel developments are also to be found in the men's wear trade, where the exclusive Jermyn Street men's wear shop may be contrasted with several multiple organisations, of which Austin Reed's shops are an example. In the latter instance, specialised knowledge again expresses itself in providing the widest possible selection and variety to suit every taste and to meet every likely demand within the price limits they have set themselves. Thus, men's shirts are offered for sale not only in a large variety of colours and qualities but in every likely combination of sleeve length and collar band. Having regard to the scale on which the operations are conducted, the personal contact between management and customer, which is such a prominent characteristic of the small exclusive speciality shop, must necessarily disappear, but plenty of scope is still left for those other important features of this kind of shop, namely, individuality and imaginative effort.

The illustrations given show that the speciality idea is capable of considerable development, and within its limited field that development is taking place along the same broad lines which retail distribution as a whole has already followed. In many cases the natural avenue of expansion for the speciality shop is into the multiple organisation, and in the women's wear trade particularly many such chains of speciality shops are to be found, as, for example, Etam's hosiery shops. Alternatively, the idea develops into the specialist store such as Liberty's or Heal's, which is organically in line with the departmental store. There are also several examples of a multiple organisation which, while maintaining a series of smaller units in other districts, focus attention on some central establishment that in scale and character challenges comparison with the departmental store. Austin Reed's Regent Street branch, and the Oxford Street branches of C. & A. Modes Ltd., and of Lilley & Skinner Ltd., are illustrations from the men's wear, women's wear and foot-wear trades respectively. Moreover, the influence of the speciality idea on the departmental store itself is not with-out significance, as there is an increasing tendency to be observed in the latter towards trying to give to each of its departments the standing and cachet of a speciality shop.

CHAPTER IV

THE DEPARTMENTAL STORE

IT has already been pointed out that the small independent shop is the basic unit of distribution, and that as soon as the productive capacity and transport facilities of the world began to expand, the expansion of the distributive unit had to follow in one of two directions—either by enlarging the size of the unit or by keeping the size of the unit the same and multiplying it in a number of different localities. The departmental store represents the first of these two alternatives, and was not only the first fundamental change in distributive methods to materialise, but, at the start, also developed more rapidly than the other large distributive organisations. The growth of most of the individual stores that are household names to-day ran roughly parallel with the development of this type of distribution, each gradually expanding as the departmental store conception became more firmly established as a type of distributive unit. There are very few examples of departmental stores as such being established in any particular locality as a result of some definite preconceived plan. In fact, nearly all the existing stores have developed by stages either from the drapery establishment or less often from the grocery shop. There are many reasons why the development should have taken this form, and why the draper in particular eventually emerged into the store proprietor. In the first place, it is generally easier to sell more goods of a related kind to the same customer than to find more customers

in a given locality to purchase the same kind of merchandise, especially where the population from which
potential customers can be drawn is limited. Secondly,
the stock which a draper keeps lends itself in a special
way to this form of expansion, in that departments
stocked with goods of a kindred character can readily be
added. Indeed, it has been suggested that the development of the departmental store from the draper's shop
is closely paralleled by, and may possibly to some extent
be due to, a similar development during the same period
in the city wholesale houses. Whether this is so or not,
the departmental store is more often a woman's store,
with special emphasis given to everything relating to
women's wear.

In an historical survey of this kind, reference must be
made, before dealing with its special technique, to the
revolution which the departmental store introduced into
distributive methods. Previous to its appearance some
sixty or seventy years ago, shopping was very largely a
matter of chaffering, and the price which a customer was
asked to pay depended largely on her appearance and the
view which the shop assistant took of what she could
afford. Indeed, shop assistants were encouraged to extract the last possible penny by being paid commission
on anything above a given price which they were successful in exacting. The departmental store is believed to
have been the first retail organisation to mark its goods
in plain figures, and this in itself was an important advance
towards reducing prices to the customer. In addition to
this, however, the store, owing to the aggregate purchasing power of its associated departments, held an enormous

advantage over its smaller competitor in being able to buy in the best market, and with the consequent increase in turnover, store prices soon came to be synonymous with low prices. Moreover, the departmental store may fairly claim to have revolutionised shopping habits as well. Until the retail unit developed on a large scale, it was a matter of some embarrassment for a potential customer to enter a shop without any special intention of making a purchase but merely to inspect and price the merchandise on display. That embarrassment would, under the conditions that previously obtained, certainly have been aggravated by importunity on the part of the sales assistant, and in consequence the rule used to be that a shop was entered only with the definite object of satisfying some specific want. That attitude has been completely altered by the standing invitation which the modern departmental store extends to every member of the public to enter and make all the price comparisons and inspections that may be desired. Hence, the fact of a customer's entry is not now assumed to be a presupposition of a desire to purchase, and there has grown up, in accordance with the technique which the store developed, the habit of visiting different departments or even different stores until the right article at the right price has been found. This represents an important addition to the shopping convenience of the public, and it is now such a recognised characteristic of everyday life that the contribution made by the departmental store to its creation is very often forgotten.

The two possible avenues of expansion mentioned above also reflect two fundamentally different avenues of approach to the customer. Wider circles of customers may be reached by establishing units of a chain in more and more shopping centres, or they may be attracted to some central location by every inducement open to the store proprietor. Many of the activities of the departmental store, which on the face of them may appear somewhat extravagant or even superfluous, cannot properly be understood unless this central fact is firmly grasped. Its whole technique, and almost its existence, depends on drawing an ever wider circle of customers from their own residential neighbourhood to shop in the principal thoroughfares of the town or city to which the store belongs. Hence a central site in the main shopping area is indispensable. Moreover, having regard to its objective, an impressive building is almost as essential as a good location for attracting both those for whom it immediately caters, and the very important floating population of visitors from the surrounding neighbourhood, the provinces, and abroad, which it also seeks to serve. The principal departmental store in a town should by the character of its building be as much an attraction to the visitor as the prominent public buildings or any other architectural feature. To be housed in dignified and impressive premises is therefore not so much an extravagance as a logical development of its technique.

In passing, reference may be made to the interest which the departmental store has for the provincial or foreign visitor. In the case of the former, the names of the leading stores are, through their use of national advertising, such household words that it is remarkable how frequently they are one of the first places to be visited.

For the foreign visitor the stores have the additional attraction that they provide the best available bird's-eye view of a country's national life, in so far as it can be reflected in the merchandise that it buys and sells. Not only in Great Britain but in other countries as well, the overwhelming proportion of merchandise on sale is of national origin, and, in consequence, by visiting the stores the foreign visitor can quickly form a fairly shrewd idea of the nation's capacity for producing merchandise normally sold through retail channels.

It follows from what has been said that much care and attention have to be given to window display, so that the passing public may be attracted inside, while within the store itself, wide gangways, lofty ceilings, handsome fittings, cheerful illumination, and an artistic display of the merchandise that is offered for sale, all combine to carry out the objective of making shopping as pleasant as possible. Furthermore, as the personal contact between the store and its customer must be made through the sales assistant, the stores generally take pains to select assistants of good type and educate them not only in the arts of salesmanship, but in the character of the merchandise they are called upon to handle.

When once the goal of the departmental store is properly appreciated, it is not difficult to understand why it devotes more attention to advertising in all its forms than do other kinds of retailing. Having only one large and expensive site from which to conduct its business, it has to exploit to the utmost all the advantages which are furnished by its central location. Thus nearly all the large departmental stores maintain mail order depart-

ments, which account for a considerable—though generally diminishing—proportion of their turnover, and
arrangements are, of course, also made for executing
orders received by telephone. It is merely a development of the same technique that delivery services are
provided, so that goods purchased in its cheerful atmosphere may be delivered to the customer's house with as
little trouble as if they had been bought in the immediate
neighbourhood. Again, although stores catering for the
popular class of trade often conduct their business wholly
on a cash basis, credit facilities are almost always provided by the stores who are engaged in the medium and
higher class trade, and such credit business may account
for as much as 80 per cent. of their total turnover.

All these services, both internal and external, which the
departmental store sets out to supply, are to be explained
by the three-fold objective of first bringing to its doors
the whole of that class of the public for which it caters,
and not merely those in its immediate neighbourhood ;
secondly, when once they are inside the store, of making
shopping as agreeable and attractive as possible ; and,
thirdly, of satisfying all reasonable shopping requirements
of which the potential customer is conscious. In achieving the third objective, the store is always limited by the
class of trade which it seeks to undertake, but within that
limitation it must maintain in each of its departments a
wide assortment of stock at different price levels, and of
sufficient variety to meet every reasonable demand. The
internal organisation by means of which these results are
achieved will be described in detail in the second section
of the book.

The departmental store as it exists to-day in this country has much in its favour as a type of distributive unit, and its relative importance in the retail structure may be measured by the fact that some three hundred stores account for possibly $7\frac{1}{2}$ per cent. of the total retail trade of the country. If success may be regarded as a criterion of efficiency, it is significant that since the time of the post-war slump up to the commencement of the existing depression, the leading departmental stores have been able to report almost uninterrupted progress, and this in spite of falling prices, unemployment and general industrial depression. Much of that success has undoubtedly been due to the skill and enterprise of the management, who have been quick to scrap out-of-date methods, try out new systems and to recognise the importance of expanding sales and rapid turnover of stocks. These factors, generally combined with progressive and persistent advertising, have enabled the stores to exploit to the utmost the outstanding advantage which they enjoy of possessing on a central site a series of possibly a hundred different retail units under the same roof. In this connection it is interesting to observe the many instances which could be quoted of how a store, or a group of stores, has by its vigorous and energetic business methods created entirely new and important shopping centres. The Barker group in Kensington, or Selfridge's in Oxford Street, are two examples which immediately come to mind.

The appeal which they are thus able to make to a wider range of customers, together with the development of a flexible merchandising technique which allows them to profit quickly by market opportunities or sudden changes in fashion or demand, has made it possible for the stores to maintain their prices at a highly competitive level, and by purchasing largely from manufacturers to pass on to the public the important economies obtained from large-scale buying. Moreover, while it shares with all large organisations the disadvantage that the personal contact between management and customer can no longer be maintained, a departmental store can, and does, have a definite personality of its own which other forms of large-scale retailing do not yet appear to have acquired to quite the same degree.

At the same time, it must be recognised that departmental store technique, like any other, suffers from the defects of its qualities, and in all parts of the world it is now being subjected to pressure by other forms of retail organisations which have developed during the last few years. It is interesting to note the effect of this competition, as it explains many of the trends which are taking place in this field to-day. Each department of a store is, in effect, a separate retail shop, and is in charge of a buyer who is normally responsible both for buying and selling the merchandise in his department. It is in many ways a wholesome and salutary check on the person who buys that he should also be made responsible for selling what he has bought. On the other hand, it may well be that a skilful buyer does not always possess the qualities of the successful salesman, while a good salesman, who can make the most of what he has to sell, may lack those elements of shrewdness and foresight which go to make up a skilful buyer. The efforts of the buyer are, of course, supplemented by the management on the one side, through the statistical control supplied by the counting-house, and on the other, by the sales promotion technique of the publicity department, but, in spite of this, it is open to question whether the combination of the buying and selling functions under one control is always a source of strength. Again, the very variety of merchandise which has to be stocked in some departments in order to achieve the objective of being the Universal Provider is, unless subject to constant and rigorous control, another source of potential weakness, especially during a period of falling prices. Although the leading stores have taken active steps in the last few years to reduce unnecessary price ranges and variations in quality and style, the ordinary multiple shop, which concentrates its attention on a narrower field, has a much easier merchandising problem to solve. Again, in another direction the development of the speciality conception has confronted the departmental store with the task of doing in each of its many departments as efficient a merchandising job as a competitor who applies the whole of his specialised knowledge to only one small section. Further, it is now not alone among retail organisations in enjoying the advantages of large-scale buying, and while the individual department may still retain its supremacy in that direction over the ordinary retail shop, it can no longer hope to compete in mere purchasing power alone with the large multiple organisations. Finally, the departmental store has constantly to contend, as will be shown in a later chapter, with a somewhat rigid expense account, in which many items are outside its control, while most show a persistent tendency to increase even when subjected to the strictest supervision. The multiple shop firms, on the other hand, with their more flexible organisation, can close unprofitable branches at will and open others on more promising sites. They have thus a great advantage in being able more readily to adjust expenses to turnover.

The departmental stores have not been slow in providing an answer to these various forms of competition. It has already been explained that certain classes of stores are now tending to regard their departments not as so many retail units but as speciality shops, and aim at giving in their departments the service which a speciality shop provides. The new Man's Shop at Harrods is a good illustration of this tendency.

The next question was to meet the competition of the multiple organisations by increasing purchasing power, and this has been achieved not so much by the expansion of the individual store as by the amalgamation of different independent units under one financial control. The result is that there are now several groups or chains of departmental stores in existence. For example, Harrods now control two other London stores, Dickins & Jones and D. H. Evans, as well as Kendal Milne in Manchester. All these four stores cater more or less for the same good-class clientele, but most of the advantages of amalgamation have been confined to the introduction of more efficient methods of management and additional capital where required, and have so far extended in only a limited degree to any system of central buying of the staple commodities which are sold in each of the stores. Different examples of the same process are the Selfridge

Provincial Stores and the Drapery Trust, but here again the difficult question of central buying is being tackled very slowly. In each of these instances some twenty to sixty stores doing different types of trade, some high, some medium, some low, have been brought under one financial control. The advantages to the amalgamation are that their interests are widely spread, and it is unlikely that all their constituent stores will show poor results at the same time. The amalgamated unit, on the other hand, has had the benefit of any additional working capital required, modernisation of premises and equipment, and the introduction where necessary of more efficient management. Signs are not wanting, however, as, for example, the institution, when practicable, of co-operative delivery services, that the great potentialities inherent in these groups will not be allowed to remain undeveloped.

The most interesting example, however, of rationalisation is presented by Messrs. Lewis's Ltd., of Liverpool, Manchester, Birmingham and Glasgow, as the methods they have adopted are unique not only in this country, but so far as is known, in the world, and may well indicate the line of development which the departmental store is likely to follow. In this instance stores of exactly the same type have been established in towns containing an industrial population of more or less the same character ; and wherever practicable the departments have been standardised, so that in the same department at each of the four stores the same staple qualities of merchandise are sold in the same assortments and at the same price levels. Allowance, of course, is also made for the necessary elasticity in individual cases. As soon as this standardisation had been completed, it was then possible for one buyer to control the buying of the same merchandise for all four stores, instead of having a separate buyer for the same department in each store. This centralisation of the buying function enabled all the economies of bulk purchasing to be enjoyed and also of course materially reduced the actual buying expense itself. The concern now buys on such a large scale that in many lines the whole process of production and distribution can be controlled from the raw material upwards, and so far as purchasing power is concerned, it is therefore enjoying all the advantages to be gained from central buying.

Having thus reorganised their buying on a central basis, attention was then concentrated on the selling activities of the individual departments. It has been seen that the buyer, who is usually in charge of the department, now confines his whole attention to buying at Lewis's central buying office in London. The general administration of the department has therefore been transferred to a departmental sales manager, whose duty it is to display his merchandise to the best advantage, instruct the sales assistants in their selling technique, arrange departmental events, and generally look after his department in the manner of the ordinary store buyer. He is in turn controlled by two people, each of whom is directly responsible to the management of the store, and has a range of departments on one or more floors under his supervision. The first is called the Sales Promoter, who is responsible for the whole of the selling side in the group under his control, for organising selling events, devising special selling schemes, selecting lines of merchandise for advertising, and for the whole of the sales promotion work generally. The other is the Stock Controller, whose business it is to see that the stock is kept moving at the required rate of stock-turn, and that the buying indents are made on the central buying office, so that the right amount and kind of stock is always maintained. In other words, the buying, selling and stock-control functions in the departments have now been placed in the hands of a specialist in each sphere, and this arrangement, while ensuring that the necessary co-ordination is achieved, disposes at once of the criticism often levelled at departmental store technique, that where the same person is responsible for different functions it is only rarely that they can all be satisfactorily performed.

CHAPTER V

THE MULTIPLE SHOP

THE second line of expansion from the small independent shop which has been taken by large-scale retailing in this country is represented by the multiple branch organisation. In this instance the retail unit, which may vary considerably in size both in the same chain and in different chains, is multiplied in a number of different shopping areas either locally or nationally, and the resulting multiple organisation is controlled by one central management. Within this genus there are three important species which will be dealt with separately.

The first is the ordinary multiple shop company which distributes merchandise covered by a single trade such as groceries, boots and shoes or stationery. The other two are the co-operative societies and the " fixed-price " chain stores, both of which somewhat resemble the departmental store in the variety of merchandise that they distribute, but in structure and organisation are in line with the multiple shop type of distribution. In this section, unless otherwise stated, attention will be directed only to the first type, namely, those multiple organisations which are connected with a particular trade.

It has been pointed out that the departmental stores in this country have made considerable strides since the war, and the same is equally true both in this country and especially in America of the multiple branch organisations. In fact, in all countries the period since the war has marked a notable advance in the development of large-scale retailing. For example, the largest retail organisation in the world—the Great Atlantic and Pacific Tea Company of the United States—was founded in 1858, and by 1912 had established 447 branches. By 1919 the number of branches had increased to 4246, and in 1930 exceeded no less than 15,500. In this country the first multiple concern was founded at about much the same time, and, as in America, was engaged in the distribution of non-perishable packeted goods, such as tea, coffee, cocoa, etc. Indeed, the grocery trade offered a peculiarly promising field for this type of organisation, and it is in this trade that it has expanded most rapidly, especially during the last twenty years. There are now more than 400 of these multiple grocery concerns, controlling in all more than 10,000 different branches. Certain of the largest of these chains have recently been amalgamated and brought under one financial control, and the combined concern represents by far the largest retail organisation in the country. According to the statement made by the chairman at the annual meeting of the Home and Colonial Stores, this combine now controls no less than 3685 shops throughout Great Britain and Ireland.

The multiple branch type of retailing has, of course, also extended to other fields, and examples are now to be found in at least twenty-five different trades. Those trades concerned with the distribution of food, such as bakers, butchers, confectioners, dairies, etc., still contain the largest number of multiple concerns. Outside food the principal trades in which they are to be found are boots and shoes, men's outfitting, stationery, and drugs.

Examples are also to be met with in what would appear at first sight to be such unlikely trades as women's fashions and furniture.

Taken as a whole, and excluding the co-operative societies and the " fixed-price " chain stores, the multiple organisations now account for a substantial proportion of the country's annual retail trade. Some forty to fifty thousand shops at least are under this type of control, and their aggregate turnover probably represents some 15 to 20 per cent. of total retail sales. Within the individual trades themselves, however, there is considerable variation in the importance which the multiple concerns enjoy. In the boot and shoe field the multiples are believed to account for probably more than 40 per cent. of the annual retail turnover, while a multiple tailoring company claim that they supply one out of every five men's suits sold in the country. The largest multiple chemist concern, with more than 900 branches, is understood to control about one-sixth of the total trade in its field, while in the aggregate the multiple grocery concerns probably control a much larger proportion.

On the other hand, sales through the multiple tobacconists are less than 1 per cent. of the total retail turnover in that trade, and multiple fruiterers and fishmongers also account for a negligible share of the sales in their respective fields.

The explanation of this phenomenon is not easy to find. At first sight it might be thought that packeted goods, such as cigarettes and chocolates, represented an ideal field for this form of distribution ; yet in neither trade do the multiple shop companies so far occupy a position

of any great importance. In these two instances the
explanation may be that the commodities in question call
for distribution through an enormous number of retail
outlets, and as the manufacturers themselves by national
advertising and by fixing retail selling prices play a large
part in controlling distribution, all that is required is
some one to hand the goods over the counter. At any
rate, by grading their trade discounts in such a way that
the inducement to purchase on a large scale is not sufficiently attractive, the manufacturers concerned seem to
have gone out of their way to encourage the distribution
of their products through the small independent retailer.
In the case of fish and fruit, the perishable nature of the
product may explain why distribution through multiple
channels is the exception rather than the rule. Whatever
may be the ultimate cause, the fact remains that in spite
of the huge advances made by multiple branch retailing
since the beginning of the century, and especially since
the war, there are no examples to be found either in this
country or elsewhere of the distribution of any commodity
or group of commodities being monopolised by this type
of organisation to the exclusion of the small shopkeeper,
and indeed it is doubtful whether even in any particular
trade they account in the aggregate for as much as 50 per
cent. of the annual retail sales.

It is more than usually difficult to make any generalisations which will apply to all kinds of multiple branch
organisations as each concern appears to be very much
a law unto itself. Even between two multiple chains in
the same trade there may be considerable variations in the
methods adopted, while in comparing two organisations

in different trades it becomes even more difficult to establish any general similarity in technique. In the last resort, however, every multiple chain represents a combination in some form or other of centralised buying with decentralised selling, and it is the task of each concern to adapt this type of organisation in the manner best suited to the circumstances of its particular trade. Indeed, it is the fundamental advantage of this form of distribution that the buying and selling functions are clearly distinguished and can be kept strictly apart. Broadly speaking, all the buying is undertaken at the centre, where the general management of the organisation resides, while everything connected with the selling of the merchandise to the public, although directed and controlled from the centre, is the responsibility of the local managers in the branches scattered throughout the country.

It is impossible to particularise in any greater detail the methods adopted in buying, as these must vary so largely with the character of the goods distributed. In some cases, as, for example, Boots, the cash chemists, a considerable variety of merchandise is kept at each branch, with possibly a range of prices in the more prominent lines to cater for different classes of customer. The root principle, however, will be found in the direction of either restricting the range of prices at which merchandise is sold, as in the case of the " fixed-price " chain stores, which will be dealt with in the next section, or of limiting the kinds of different merchandise sold, as in the case of the Home and Colonial Stores. There are obvious advantages to be gained in bulking purchasing power at a few prices, or on relatively few lines, and these questions of policy are, of course, determined from the central office. So far as the branch is concerned, it is seldom that the local manager has any authority to buy, although in the case of the larger branches of W. H. Smith & Son Ltd., and in certain other chains, it is understood that power is given to the manager to cover requirements locally for a limited amount of merchandise. The local branch is often used to test out in different areas the public demand for new merchandise, and when that demand has been ascertained, bulk orders for the whole of the organisation are placed centrally; and the task of the local manager is to control the merchandise of his branch in such a way that the goods supplied to him from the central warehouse are displayed and offered for sale generally to the best possible advantage. Where the number of branches controlled may exceed three figures, it can be appreciated that the concentration of all this buying power for any individual line in the hands of one central buyer provides him with a unique opportunity for securing the maximum economies; and in fact both in this country and in America the orders he is able to place direct with the manufacturers are far larger than those of many wholesalers. Indeed, the multiple organisation generally performs the function both of warehouseman and retailer, but, of course, this means that while enjoying the advantages of bulk buying it also has to incur the costs of warehousing until the goods reach the shelves of the individual branches.

This concentration of purchasing power, and the huge orders to which it gives rise, leads naturally to the question of vertical as well as horizontal combination. In other words, the multiple firm may be encouraged to manufacture for itself those staple articles for which it can provide a steady market. There is also an urge to this vertical organisation from the other direction, in the sense that manufacturers may find themselves compelled to control a distributive organisation in order to provide an assured retail outlet for their product. However, from whichever direction the initiative comes, the combination of the multiple distributive organisation and manufacturing activities is by no means uncommon, although the relative importance of the two factors may vary considerably in different trades, and even between two concerns in the same trade. At the one end of the scale there is the Singer Sewing Machine Company Ltd., which itself produces all the machines that are sold through its 900 retail outlets, while the multiple tailors, such as Montague Burton, also supply examples of a manufacturing organisation providing the bulk, if not all, of the merchandise distributed through their retail branches. The boot and shoe trade contains two excellent illustrations of both tendencies. In the one case Freeman Hardy & Willis Ltd., who were originally manufacturers, opened a chain of retail shops in different parts of the country as outlets for their increased productive output. To-day over 500 branches are operated under the name of this concern, and although it was originally a manufacturing business, only a comparatively small proportion of the merchandise sold in their retail shops is now of their own manufacture. The second case is that of J. Sears & Co. (Trueform) Ltd., who operate over 700 branches and have always been distributors; however, they now control a considerable manufacturing business as well, in order to provide supplies to some extent for their retail outlets. Both these concerns are now under the same control, but their history illustrates the tendency for production and multiple distribution to combine into a joint organisation.

Many other examples of this combination could be quoted from, say, the food or chemist trades, but it is doubtful how far this vertical type of organisation is economically sound and likely to extend. The ultimate aim of the co-operative movement is presumably an all-embracing combination of this kind. The " fixed-price " chain stores, on the other hand, appear to make it almost a fundamental practice not to undertake the manufacture of any of the merchandise which they distribute. On the whole it would appear that unless the goods are strictly of a staple or standard character, like sewing machines, the disadvantages of a vertical combination outweigh the advantages. At a period of rising prices it may well be that larger profits are to be secured by being in a position to manufacture a substantial proportion of the merchandise which is distributed through the multiple retail organisations. When prices are falling, however, there is definitely a danger that the retail outlets may be forced to accept the output of the productive factors at prices which might jeopardise the rapid distribution that is required, and at all times there is the risk that the factory may not be able to supply the right kind of merchandise at the right prices and in the right quantities, or adapt itself quickly enough to changing demand. In other words, if the connection between production and distribution is too close, and the retail outlets are compelled to stock only such merchandise as the factory produces, the assortment they will be able to offer for sale may be too small or wrongly built up or in some other way out of touch with the current public demand. There is the additional danger that a strike or a fire at the factory may throw the whole organisation out of gear.

The multiple chain has the great advantage of flexibility in that it can establish a branch in every shopping centre that appears to offer a promising market. That market may be provided in the West End of London or those central points in the suburbs of London and in the large provincial towns where important groups of shops tend to congregate, or else in shopping thoroughfares that are in close proximity to residential neighbourhoods. To secure the right site is, therefore, as important for the branch of a multiple chain as it is for a departmental store, and there is consequently great competition between multiple branch organisations, not only in the same trade but in different trades, to acquire the best positions in the popular shopping centres. Such competition incidentally tends to increase rents in the neighbourhood both for the multiple companies and for the small independent retailer ; and as rent is generally a much more important item to the latter than it is for the multiple concerns, who may be able to level out the rents they pay over a number of units in different parts of the country, this consideration makes it still more difficult for the small man, if he decides to remain where he is, to compete with his multiple rival. After the site has been selected, the size and character of the branch varies with almost every multiple company. In many cases, as for example the Home and Colonial Stores, a definite attempt is made to standardise the unit, as regards not only the external shop front, but also the internal layout and the fixtures and equipment which are installed. Where such a standardisation is practicable, there is no doubt that important economies and other advantages are to be secured in this direction. Uniformity of layout renders possible standardisation of stocks, of cash and other systems, common forms of window display, and generally simplifies the management of the unit and its control from the central office. Moreover, external uniformity has a substantial advertising value as the appearance of the individual branch comes to be associated in the public's mind with the name of the multiple concern, and this is of great importance when new branches are opened.

At the other end of the scale there are such organisations as Boots and W. H. Smith's, where although there is a degree of external uniformity which renders the individual branches readily recognisable, the different units vary considerably both in size and almost in character. Some branches are strictly utilitarian in their outward appearance, and do not attempt more than to achieve the purpose for which they were intended. Others, such as the Regent Street and Bond Street branches of Boots, have a definite æsthetic appeal, and while possibly they may be of an experimental character, the merchandise offered for sale in them seems to have quite a different cachet from that offered at their other branches. In between these two limits there are many gradations, but a common combination is that which has already been referred to in the case of the speciality chains, namely, the maintenance of one or more distinctly larger units in the West End of London with a number of smaller branches in the rest of London or in other parts of the country.

This leads to the question of advertising, where again policies vary very considerably. As a whole the multiple branch organisation does not advertise extensively, or at any rate to anything like the same extent as the departmental store. There has been a greater tendency, however, in the last few years for multiple concerns to conduct advertising campaigns, of which Boots, Lilley & Skinner, and some of the food combines may serve as illustrations. In this connection, there are good grounds for holding that advertising in the national press can be undertaken even more economically by the multiple concern than by the ordinary departmental store. In the first place, the expense can be spread over a large number of branches instead of being concentrated on a single site. Secondly, the goods advertised can be bought at their branches in possibly fifty or more different towns. On the other hand, outside its ordinary shopping radius, the departmental store has to depend on mail orders to make its advertising fully productive.

On the question of staff, the ordinary multiple company seems to fall midway between the departmental store and the " fixed-price " chain store. The departmental store assistant must really be a salesman with some technical knowledge of the merchandise he is selling, and as has been explained, the leading stores now take steps to train their sales-people accordingly. In the " fixed-price " chain store the assistant does, and is intended to do, little more than take cash and pack up the goods purchased. The more progressive multiple unit, however, generally aims at giving the same measure of personal service that would be expected from the independent retailer or the speciality shop, and some multiple concerns, such as the United Dairies and W. H. Smith, are now taking steps to give their assistants technical instruction in so far as geographical and other difficulties permit. Both in staff training and in keeping control from the central office of stocks and cash at the branches, the multiple organisation has a much more difficult task than the departmental store. In so far as any generalisation on the latter points is possible, the tendency is for each unit to have a standard stock ; and for that stock and for all additional merchandice which is booked to him at selling prices, the local manager has to account every week, or at even shorter intervals, either in cash or in kind. Further control from the centre is supplied by inspectors. The main responsibility, however, of the local manager is to concentrate on selling. He therefore has to see that his stock is kept as closely as possible in touch with local demand, and so far as an essentially impersonal organisation will permit, to give that individual selling service which is the main advantage of his small independent competitor.

CHAPTER VI

WHEN the Co-operative Movement comes to be considered, reliable statistics are at last available from which some conclusions can be drawn. As the great majority of co-operative societies are registered under the Industrial Provident Societies Acts, statutory returns have to be made to the Chief Registrar of Friendly Societies, and a great deal of statistical information is available through his report. Very full statistics are also published by the Co-operative Union, to which nearly all the co-operative societies belong and which is the counterpart of the recognised Trade Association.

The Co-operative Movement now embraces a large number of different activities, including, among others, banking, insurance, printing and farming, in addition to distribution and production, but the distributive function, which was the first to be undertaken, continues to be the most important. In 1930 there were some 1250 retail distributive societies, whose aggregate sales amounted to over £217,000,000 [1]; on the wholesale, which includes also the productive side, the combined sales of the English and Scottish Co-operative Wholesale Societies were about £103,000,000. The share capital is contributed by members, whose holdings must not exceed a maximum of £200, and on this capital interest at the rate of 5 per cent. is paid. In 1930 the retail

[1] In 1931 this figure fell to £210,000,000.

societies had a membership of roughly 6,400,000, while the share, loan and reserve capital amounted to £142,000,000. The characteristic feature, however, of co-operative trading is the payment to its members, apart from interest on the share capital, of a dividend on the amount of purchases made during the year, and this may either be taken out in cash or left with the society to accumulate in the form of share capital. In 1930, an aggregate surplus, before deducting share interest, of just under £27,000,000 was recorded by the retail societies, and of this, over £20,000,000, or an average of 1s. 10½d. in the £, was distributed by way of dividends on sales.

The retail distributive societies, like other forms of large-scale retailing, have been steadily expanding since 1923, and although sales have not again reached the high level of £245,000,000 recorded in the boom year of 1920, there has been an uninterrupted rise both in membership and sales since 1923, and the aggregate turnover for which these societies are responsible must now represent from 12 to 15 per cent. of the country's annual retail trade. The retail societies vary considerably in size, and though a certain amount of amalgamation has been in progress during the last few years, in 1929 sixty-five societies still represented more than 50 per cent. of the total membership, while over five hundred and thirty societies, with under 1000 members each, accounted for only 3·8 per cent. of the membership. The largest societies are the London and the Royal Arsenal, Woolwich, with 394,000 and 240,000 members respectively, and although the movement still has its strongest hold in the north of England, where it first began, it is in and around London that the greatest expansion has recently taken place. Indeed, the London societies have more than doubled their membership in the last five years.

In this connection it has to be remembered that although it is customary to talk of the Co-operative Movement as if all its activities were directed by one governing executive, each society is in fact quite a separate and independent entity, and is entitled to conduct its affairs in the way its managing committee thinks fit. Thus, it would be misleading to regard the retail societies on the one hand, and the wholesale societies on the other, as forming together that kind of vertical combination which was referred to in connection with the multiple branch organisation. The connection between the two sides of the movement appears to be sufficiently loose to justify presidential statements at a co-operative congress deploring the fact that " more than one-third of the goods retailed in the societies' stores came from non-co-operative sources, and that the great majority of the societies appeared content to act as distributing agencies for goods produced by their business rivals." The capital of the wholesale societies is all held by the retail societies, by whom they were established in the first instance, but it is perfectly open to the individual retail society to purchase as it thinks fit from the wholesale society or from some other wholesale source. In fact, the larger a retail society develops, the less dependent it appears to become on the wholesale societies ; and this phenomenon is illustrated by the tendency of the larger retail societies to establish their own productive factories, although it is true that these productive activities concentrate upon fields such as baking and slaughtering, in which the wholesale societies are not strongly represented.

Although co-operative trading has now extended to such substantial dimensions, its fundamental characteristics must not be lost sight of, as they have naturally shaped the course of its development. The essential principles of the consumers' societies are that the members of the society should provide the necessary capital for setting up a shop, from which they as consumers can purchase their everyday requirements, and that, after paying interest on the share capital, any surplus not retained in the business as a reserve for development, should be returned to the members in the shape of a dividend or discount in proportion to the purchases which they had made during the year. The management of the shop is put in the hands of a committee elected from among the body of consumers by whom the society was formed, whether or not the individual members of the committee are qualified for that task by capacity or previous experience. It is this characteristic of mutuality that, combined with the limitation of individual share holdings, has exempted co-operative societies from taxation on their profits, and that exemption has doubtless contributed materially to the expansion that has taken place. On the other hand, the somewhat haphazard method of electing the management committee made it unlikely that it would contain the best managerial ability for conducting the affairs of the society; and it is only within recent years that the movement, and in particular the larger societies, have come to appreciate the value of adequately paid executives.

As the individual societies grew, it was inevitable that the element of mutuality which bound one member to another should become weaker and retreat more and more into the background. The societies themselves no longer pretend to confine their sales to members only, and indeed tender for public contracts and endeavour to attract outside custom as far as they can by advertising and in other ways.

Conversely, the individual members do not appear by any means to restrict their purchases to the co-operative society to which they belong ; and in this connection it may be something more than a coincidence that the " fixed-price " chain stores in the neighbourhood are accustomed to report increased turnover immediately after the distribution of a co-operative dividend. Another aspect of this same phenomenon may be the sharp fall since 1920, which cannot wholly be accounted for by the fall in prices, in the average sales per co-operative member. In 1930 it was £33·94 against the peak of £56·42 in the boom year of 1920. Moreover, the movement itself is no longer expanding through the creation of more societies on the original co-operative model ; on the contrary, it has already been pointed out that the tendency during the last few years has been to eliminate unnecessary competition between societies and to reduce their number by a process of amalgamation. It is rather to the absorption by the larger societies of business undertakings that had previously been in private ownership that the expansion of recent years has been due.

An individual society may have one or a number of branches, but, of course, it is only the larger societies that possess the structure of the typical multiple branch organisation which is now under consideration. In those cases, however, where the same society controls a chain of shops, there appears to be little uniformity about the individual units, as these have generally been added by a process of haphazard absorption rather than built up according to some well-defined plan. In fact they vary considerably in size from single or double shops to large establishments that may well be included in the departmental store category. There has been a noticeable tendency of late to improve both the size and the appearance of the individual unit, and more up-to-date methods of window display and interior equipment are being adopted. The much greater attention that is being paid to advertising has already been referred to, and indeed the continuous increase in membership during the last eight years has generally been attributed to the intensive propaganda that has been undertaken.

Contributory factors have been the extension of credit through hire-purchase schemes and the adoption by some societies of the so-called club system of trading, which will be described later; although both these developments are apparently regarded with some misgiving in certain sections of the movement.

So far as the merchandise sold is concerned, the retail societies were originally concerned almost wholly with the distribution of food, and, even to-day, food represents some 80 per cent. of their total sales. Here, again, possibly as a result of the absence of any uniformity in the size of the different branches, there is no question of any standardised stock, in the sense that that term would be applied in a " fixed-price " chain store, and the variety of merchandise offered for sale seems to vary very much with the character and size of the unit. However, the larger units now cover practically the same ground as the ordinary departmental store, and pay as much attention to men's and women's clothing, furniture, hardware, etc., as they do to food. Those societies that have the multiple branch structure are understood also to organise their buying on a central basis.

In regard to prices, the Rochdale pioneers decided that they would sell to their members at ordinary market prices, and it was in this that they differed fundamentally from previous attempts at co-operation, when distribution at cost price had generally been the object. Subsequently, co-operative prices have seldom been much lower and are occasionally higher than those of other well-organised retail distributors, and, indeed, price, as such, has never been the main plank of the co-operative platform. That ultimately is constituted by the ideal of co-operation, and the very potent attraction of the dividend or discount on purchases. It is in this ideal, and in the dividend, especially during a period of high prices, that the appeal of the movement to the purchasing public largely consists. Even if the retail societies, taken as a whole, decided to attempt a price appeal, it is doubtful whether their buying methods are such as to secure for them the economies of large-scale buying which are indispensable if any substantial reduction in selling prices is to be made. Although the combined sales of the

retail societies amounted in 1930 to the formidable figure
of £217,000,000, it must be remembered that this is
shared between some 1250 independent societies, so that
while the few large societies may each do a substantial
trade, the average turnover per society is under £175,000.
When this figure is split up among different categories
of merchandise, it clearly does not represent in the case
of the average individual society any substantial purchasing power in a particular category. It has already
been explained that the wholesale societies are not in a
position to bulk orders from the different retail societies,
but must rely for support on their purchasing loyalty,
and in fact supply only two-thirds of the merchandise
which the retail societies sell. Hence so long as the
wholesale and retail societies are all independent self-
contained units, not only is it impossible for the potentialities of bulk-buying within the movement to be fully
exploited, but also the individual society is generally at
a disadvantage from the point of view of purchasing
power as compared with the branches of the larger retail
undertakings under private enterprise. On the other
hand, selling expenses are not materially different from
those of any other large-scale organisation, so that while
the deduction of the dividend may eventually have the
effect of reducing the selling price, it is not on the original
level of their selling prices that the co-operative societies
rely for their competitive power.

In setting out the above facts and considerations, it
has not been overlooked that some of the individual
retail societies are exceedingly large organisations. The
London Co-operative Society, for example, has an annual

turnover of £10,000,000, while that of the Royal Arsenal, Woolwich, exceeds £7,000,000. There are many others that have sales of over £1,000,000 per annum. Such figures, of course, enable these societies to purchase on highly competitive terms. They do not, however, affect the point already touched on that the larger a retail society develops, the smaller appears to become the proportion of its total purchases that are made from the wholesale societies, and hence the potentialities inherent in the large annual turnover of the retail societies are not being, and as the movement is at present organised, cannot be fully exploited.

That the movement is alive to this wasteful duplication of effort is evidenced by the fact that trade advisory committees or associations have recently been set up for such commodities as milk and coal, in the distribution of which the societies play an important part. The express object of these associations, of which others will doubtless be established, is to prevent over-lapping within the movement and to secure that degree of unity which has been achieved through amalgamation outside the movement, so that all stages of production and distribution can be effectively controlled right through to the consumer. Another significant development in the same direction is that the wholesale societies have recently been given powers to set up retail societies of their own, but it is not clear to what extent those powers have so far been exercised.

CHAPTER VII

THE " FIXED-PRICE " CHAIN STORE

" Fixed-price " chain store is an American term used to describe the Woolworth type of organisation, and as that system of distribution is essentially an American product, the term may be retained to distinguish this from other kinds of multiple branch organisation. While for the time being the " fixed-price " chain store appears to have reached its zenith in the United States, where it originated, it is still developing rapidly in this country and even to a greater extent in Germany. In this country it is peculiarly associated with the name of Woolworth's, who now control some 450 branches and restrict their selling prices to 3d. or 6d. The system has been further developed by Marks & Spencer, who have largely extended its possibilities by increasing their price limit to 5s. The significance of this is that chain-store methods of buying and distribution are applied by this firm to a vast number of articles which are outside the scope of Woolworth's, and in addition to the ordinary articles of domestic use Marks & Spencer's stocks now include drapery and clothing, men's outfitting, boots and shoes, fancy jewellery, etc. This chain now controls some 150 branches and is still rapidly expanding. Other chains are also being started, such as the British Home Stores, which more closely resemble the Woolworth model.

The " fixed-price " chain store carries the multiple conception to its logical conclusion, and the general principles of its organisation can, therefore, be more easily defined. It seems to represent the nearest approach that has yet been attempted to mass distribution on mass production lines, and indeed requires mass production as its logical counterpart. Selling prices are deliberately restricted to the lower price-levels because at those levels mass distribution is most easily achieved. Even at these low-price ranges it selects only those lines in each different category of merchandise for which there is evidence of a large actual or potential public demand, and which call for the minimum of selling effort. It therefore dispenses automatically with the more expensive merchandise which is at once more sensitive to both price and style fluctuation and so more liable to cause loss unless rapidly sold ; moreover, such goods require a larger selection to provide a more effective choice. This standardisation both of price and of merchandise leads naturally to far greater possibilities of central buying, and of securing the closest possible prices by passing to manufacturers a steady stream of substantial orders. In addition, as all chain stores work on a cash basis, they are in a position to pay prompt cash to their suppliers and so take full advantage of all cash discounts. On the other hand, when these contacts with production have been made, it is only through some multiple branch organisation that the huge potential output of cheap articles, in which the chain store specialises, can be effectively distributed to the public.

The " fixed-price " chain store buys all its merchandise centrally. Indeed their success is largely due to the close contact which they keep with manufacturers, and owing to the size of the orders they are able to place, control can be maintained, to an extent that is beyond the reach of most other types of distributive organisation, over all stages of production from the raw material upwards. It is only by the most careful scrutiny of costings at the different stages of production that more and more articles can be brought within their self-imposed price limits. The chain stores are such large individual buyers that they can control the output of whole factories, and where a satisfactory contact of this kind is once made, it generally proves of considerable advantage to both parties, the chain store having a reliable source for its supplies and the manufacturer a steady stream of large orders to keep his machinery employed. Moreover, a manufacturer selling to a chain store has the great additional advantage that he knows he must confine his offers to a definite price range, while the task of the buyer is also greatly facilitated because his field of selection and elimination is narrowed down to a much smaller compass. On the other hand, it is significant that with one or two very minor exceptions the chain store has consciously avoided the kind of vertical combination described in connection with other types of multiple organisation, and generally considers that its purpose can best be served by preserving complete freedom of choice in the sources from which it purchases its supplies. Indeed some chain stores carry this principle to the point of refusing to take the whole output of a factory on the ground of the dangers involved both to themselves and to the manufacturers of relying too much on a single source of supply.

That the low-price limit does not unduly restrict the

variety of merchandise which a chain store is able to offer for sale may be illustrated by the fact that the Woolworth organisation in America sells no less than 10,000 different lines of goods ; while some figures quoted by Mr. Simon Marks in a recent speech confirm the huge volume of merchandise which now passes into consumption through the chain-store channel. He then mentioned that in 1930-31, Marks & Spencer sold through their branches 5½ million pairs of artificial silk stockings, 6 million ladies' undergarments, 2 million jumpers and 1 million dresses. These figures are very impressive when compared with those of any other type of distributive organisation concerned in such merchandise.

On the selling side as well the " fixed-price " chain store presents a much more definite and precise picture than the ordinary multiple branch organisation. The principles of standardisation applied so successfully to the merchandise distributed and to the prices at which it is sold, are extended to the architecture of the branches, their external appearance and internal layout all possessing a characteristic similarity. In size as well the individual branches are standardised so far as local circumstances permit, with the exception that those situated in the centre of London are considerably larger than the rest, and in point of scale almost approach the departmental store category. Internally the equipment installed is generally of a uniform character, and everything in the shape of decorative appeal is sacrificed to bare efficiency and low cost. The open-store method is almost always adopted for displaying the goods, and the layout of the counter so arranged that the customer can see and handle everything that is for sale. Although the price can only vary within narrow limits, conspicuous notices usually indicate at what price the different groups of merchandise are to be sold. As this merchandise has been selected in the first instance with the object that it should largely sell itself, and as further the whole interior layout of the store has been planned to simplify the selling process, it will be seen that there is very little left for the sales assistant to do but to handle cash and wrap up the merchandise that has been sold. Her function has been made to approach so closely to the automatic machine that it can easily be performed by inexpensive labour, and in fact it may be one of the potential sources of danger and weakness in chain-store technique that the selling staff is of a kind to which a low scale of remuneration is, and need be, paid. Advertising of a price-appeal character would clearly be out of place, as the public are already well aware that that is the basis on which chain-store merchandising rests, and in fact such advertising as may be undertaken is restricted to occasional insertions in the press announcing the opening of a new branch or the addition of some prominent new line to the merchandise on sale. Apart from effective lighting to create a cheerful atmosphere in the shop, and some care in dressing the windows, the only extraneous shopping inducement held out to the public consists in the periodical offer of certain goods at below cost price. Every form of personal service and decorative attraction in the shape of elaborate fittings or colourful wrappings is reduced to a minimum, although as an illustration of how different types of distribution tend to merge into one another, it is interesting to note that even the " fixed-price " chain store will now in certain cases undertake delivery if purchases exceed a certain amount.

CHAPTER VIII

THE CHARACTERISTICS OF MULTIPLE ORGANISATIONS

ALTHOUGH the " fixed-price " chain stores have definite characteristics which are peculiar to themselves, they give on the whole the clearest picture of multiple shop technique, and in order to avoid unnecessary duplication, it may be convenient to discuss the merits of this type of distribution with particular reference to them. It should be clearly understood, however, that any expressions used must be applied in a modified form to the ordinary multiple concern which operates within a single trade. Although the latter may not as yet have exploited to the full all the advantages that lie to hand in its organisation, yet at the same time it is immune from many of the dangers and disadvantages to which the " fixed-price " chain store is or may be subject.

The main advantage of the " fixed-price " chain stores lies in the fact that they have carried the principles of simplification and standardisation to their logical limit, and by making a really effective job of central buying are able so to control machine-power that goods can be produced at prices previously out of reach. It is true, of course, that by purchasing direct from the manufacturer they have to perform the functions of both warehouseman and retailer, and that therefore warehousing rent and charges have to be offset against some of the economies that are secured ; nor is this source of additional expense wholly removed by arranging for delivery from the manufacturer direct to the branches rather than to some central warehouse.

At the same time, their selling technique has been brought into line with their buying methods, and every unnecessary frill has been eliminated so as to reduce selling costs to the barest minimum. There are no counting house expenses in connection with customer credit, while delivery and advertising charges, where they exist at all, are negligible in comparison with total sales. Although their total expenses are for that reason probably lower than those of any other retail organisation, there can be little doubt that their ability to sell cheaply is influenced to a much larger extent by being able to control mass production than by low selling costs. In turn, the higher rate of stock-turn which these methods render inevitable, ensures that capital is not being left unprofitably employed in idle stock. Moreover, the conscious effort to sell as cheaply as possible does not mean that the profit on each transaction is necessarily a small one, and, indeed, on a percentage basis the gross margin on many 3d. and 6d. lines is probably as large as any retailer could hope to expect on more expensive merchandise. That a " fixed-price " chain store is a highly profitable proposition is evidenced by the recently published profits of Woolworth's, which, in 1931, with a chain in this country of some 450 shops, exceeded £4,200,000, or more than twice as much as the profits in the same year of the largest bank in the world. Marks & Spencer also have reported a phenomenal growth in profits since 1925.

At the same time it must not be forgotten that general conditions have been exceptionally favourable for the development of this kind of distribution ; nor does the striking success already achieved necessarily mean that development will be equally rapid in the future. After an almost uninterrupted growth up to 1928, chain stores in America have since reported declines in their sales, and there are other indications that in that country future progress is not going to be easy. In Great Britain and on the Continent, on the other hand, the " fixed-price " chain store is still exploiting what is largely a virgin market, and the sense of novelty which it gives to the shopping public has not yet worn off. Secondly, a period of falling prices is always favourable to chain-store distribution, as they are able to bring a wider variety of merchandise within their " fixed-price " limits, and also because in times of depression the retailer who specialises in the cheaper quality merchandise always has the benefit not only of his own regular customers but also of those classes which in more prosperous times would prefer more expensive goods. Conversely, high prices, and in particular a rapid and substantial rise in prices such as occurred during and just after the war, tend to render more difficult the technique of the " fixed-price " store.

Moreover, the principle on which chain-store merchandising rests is the elimination of all slow-selling merchandise, and concentration on those goods which most people have been found to want. These principles undoubtedly facilitate bulk-purchasing and low prices, but there comes a point when the customer objects to being regarded as a standardised unit and being offered standardised merchandise at a standard price. The desire to possess something which is not quite the same as that worn or used by the bulk of the population is deeply ingrained in human nature, and although it does not apply in the same degree to many of the staple articles in which the chain store specialises, the personal touch is still and always will be an important factor in re-tailing.   The experience of Henry Ford with Model T suggests that even the most efficient standardised result of mass-production methods may lose its appeal to the public in spite of its low price; and although that point has certainly not been reached yet in this country, it may be asked whether the same experience will not ultimately overtake chain-store distribution.

Again, in the case of the chain store, the relationship between shop and customer is probably less personal than in that of any other form of distribution, and its whole technique makes it very difficult to capture any part of that personality which is so great an advantage to the speciality shop and departmental store.

This disadvantage may help to explain the extraordin-ary hostility which chain stores seem to have provoked against themselves in other countries where they have been established.   For example, in Germany the Govern-ment have recently issued a decree that for the next two years no more chain store branches are to be established in towns of under 100,000 inhabitants.   In the United States all multiple branch organisations, including " fixed-price " chain stores, have been made subject in certain States to special forms of taxation from which other types of retail distribution are exempt.   Now it may be true that this agitation has been largely promoted by the in-dependent retailer, who doubtless felt acutely the effects of chain-store competition, but it is also true that such agitation does not reach the stage of legislative discrimination unless it has to some degree the powerful backing of public opinion. It is, therefore, somewhat curious to observe how in two different countries this type of organisation has apparently been singled out for Government attack, and how the public have associated themselves with the contentions of the independent retailer in his campaign against the multiple concern. These protests generally take the form that as the whole of the profits made by the multiple branch are sent out of the town or district to some central point where the head office is established, the town is being deprived of its capital resources, and there is little identity of interest between the branch and the locality in which it is situated. In this country there are as yet only a few examples of the " fixed-price " chain store type of distribution, but as competition between them develops, and the objections outlined above become accentuated, it will be interesting to observe if any similar animosity is engendered here, or whether there will be the same reaction on the part of the public against price-appeal alone in favour of more comfortable shopping conditions and a wider selection from which to purchase, even at a slightly higher price.

CHAPTER IX

CLUB TRADING

A SHORT description may here be given of what is known as Club Trading, which is a prominent feature of retailing among the poorer population of the chief industrial areas. This type of trading assumes two forms :—

(*a*) Clubs into which a member pays weekly deposits, receiving interest on those deposits, and using both principal and interest at the end of an agreed period to make purchases at some specified shop or shops.

(*b*) Those in which the member may receive the goods he wants to buy before he has actually completed payment for them.

The first type probably owes its origin to the Thrift or Clothing Clubs that were organised in connection with some Church or Chapel, and in which the member was not permitted to make purchases against the total value of his deposits until the club books were made up at the end of a specified period. The principle, however, was soon taken over by enterprising retailers, who organised schemes of a similar kind in connection with their own shops. They extended the scope by throwing it open to the public generally, and added various attractions, such as permission to purchase against the deposits before the club book had been made up.

The second type is much the more important of the two, and has much in common with the ordinary principles of hire-purchase trading. This type again takes two main forms. Under one system some approved person, who is called the Club Holder, and who is quite independent of the business in connection with which the club is run, persuades, say, twenty persons to join his club, and to pay him an amount of, e.g. 1s. every week. At the end of the week the club holder pays in to his principals the amount he has collected, namely £1, and in return receives a voucher for the same value. This is balloted for among the subscribers, and it can then be exchanged for goods valued at £1 from the concern by which the club is sponsored. The same process occurs every week for twenty weeks, when every member will have received goods in exchange for the total of the weekly payments he has made, and the club comes to an end. The club holder is paid for his services by the sponsoring firm on a commission basis of generally 7½ per cent. on the amount he has collected. This is possibly the commonest form of club trading, and is adopted not only by the co-operative societies, but also by many departmental stores that cater for the lower end of the trade in the suburbs of London and in the provinces.

The other system is that adopted by such concerns as the Provident Clothing Club, the Bristol Clothing Club, and many others of a similar type. They operate through canvassers and agents, and issue vouchers to approved customers for amounts which vary according to individual requirements. If the voucher is for £1 it is issued to the member on payment of the first instalment of 1s., together with poundage at the rate of 1s. in the £. The balance is paid in nineteen weekly instalments of 1s., and as soon as the first payment has been made the voucher can be exchanged for goods at certain specified shops with which the clothing club has come to an arrangement. The collector is paid on a commission basis of about $7\frac{1}{2}$ per cent. on the money he collects, while the clothing club extracts a discount from the retailer of between 15 and $17\frac{1}{2}$ per cent. for the business which it introduces to him. A member of the club, on the other hand, enjoys the ordinary benefits of hire-purchase trading. As a variation of this type, the club may be run not by an independent financial corporation like those mentioned above, but by the store at which its vouchers can be exchanged for goods.

This whole system of club trading is very much more widespread than is generally imagined, and in the large industrial districts very often represents the only method by which the poorer class of customer can obtain credit. To this extent those sections of the retail trade which encourage it are doing something to ease the path of the poorer community, and having regard to the economic circumstances of the people who take advantage of the facilities provided, the percentage of bad debts incurred is surprisingly low. On the other hand, the figures which have been mentioned are sufficient to indicate that the purchaser generally has to pay a heavy price for the credit which is extended to him, and from the point of view of the retail or other concern which sponsors the club, the percentage cost of the business introduced in this way must tend to keep expenses high. Frequently, therefore, it only proves an economic proposition in so far as the additional turnover created makes a substantial contribution towards the general overheads which the rest of the business has to bear.

CHAPTER X

MAIL ORDER BUSINESS

THE only other form of retailing which calls for consideration is the mail order business. In this case the potential customer for one reason or another is in a position neither to see nor handle the actual merchandise, and so the selling appeal has to be made to him by post, through the medium of catalogues and press advertisements, and where practicable also by small samples. The mail order organisation is more particularly an American development of the late nineteenth century, for in that country the enormous distances involved made the outlying districts more or less dependent on this type of trading. Cheap postage and carriage are presuppositions of its development, combined at a subsequent stage with a wide circulation of the national press. Its technique is, of course, quite different from that of other forms of retailing. As there is no question of displaying the merchandise, it can dispense with elaborate shop fronts and interior equipment, and does not have to pay high rents for suitable locations in good shopping areas. The situation of the warehouse from which the business is conducted is immaterial, provided it is convenient for rail and other transport facilities ; and the process of handling the order from the time the letter enclosing it is received until the goods are finally despatched can be carried out with a less expensive type of labour than is required, for example, in the selling staff of a departmental store. Moreover, the large mail order business has one great advantage over every other form of retailing. Although it is subject to seasonal variations, it is not quite so much at the mercy of shopping habits and can make arrangements to ensure an even flow of pressure on its staff and space. The peaks and valleys of customer demand during the course of the day, which is a major factor in keeping expenses high in the ordinary retail establishment, do not arise to the same degree in the mail order business, where organisation and experience can readily adapt available resources to all normal demands upon them.

Nevertheless, so far as selling costs as a whole are concerned, it is doubtful whether there is very much difference as compared with other forms of retailing. The additional cost of printing, advertising, postage, warehousing rent and charges, and the returns of merchandise sent on approval, probably cancel out the economies enjoyed in other directions.

It is more on the buying side that savings can be effected. Although the variety of merchandise included in the huge catalogue of the large American houses is very wide, the field that can be conveniently covered by a mail order trade is necessarily restricted, and for the lines selected within that field the mail order house can get very close prices by placing large orders direct with manufacturers. In the case of staple commodities, for which it can rely on a steady demand of measurable size, this type of distribution should have an advantage on price, but it must be remembered that it is always buying some distance ahead, for a problematical demand which may or may not materialise, and once the merchandise has been bought, and the catalogues have been printed, the mail order house cannot so readily adjust its prices or its qualities as the ordinary retail shop. It cannot be sure that it is offering the right selection or that its qualities and designs are right ; nor can it compete effectively on fashion appeal. Thus any organisation that is dependent on the periodical issue of a catalogue is peculiarly vulnerable to falling prices, and in particular to a sudden slump, such as that which occurred after the post-war boom.

Owing to the much shorter distances to be considered, the mail order business has not developed in this country to anything like the extent that it has in the United States, where the large houses, such as Sears Roebuck and Montgomery Ward, distribute an astonishing variety and volume of merchandise in this way. Even in America, however, mail order sales have been showing a steady decline over the last few years, and the two leading concerns have recently established chains of departmental and other stores to supplement their original mail order trade. In this country there are few firms who do nothing else but a general mail order business ; some concerns combine mail order with club trade, as described in the previous section, but the largest trade of this kind is probably done through the mail order departments of the departmental stores. In their case it is the natural corollary of their intensive press advertising, and helps to bring some return from that part of the newspaper circulation they pay for in their advertising rates, which is outside the radius of personal shopping.

The mail order type of distribution certainly performs a definite function in supplying the wants of people in outlying districts or of restricted mobility, but clearly has its limitations in that a purchaser, if he can, always prefers to examine personally the article he wants to buy, and to exercise a choice among a selection of merchandise which he can see and handle. The development of the internal combustion engine and the enormous increase of road transport since the war, which has brought outlying districts closer to shopping areas, combined with the improvement that has taken place in provincial retailing methods, have inevitably had a detrimental effect on mail order trade, and fully account for the contraction in sales. While it is certain that it will not wholly disappear, it seems probable, from the experience both in this country and in the United States, that except as an adjunct to personal shopping, mail order trading will in future be a declining factor in the distributive system.

Section 2. The Departmental Store in Action

CHAPTER XI

THE BUILDING

THE real usefulness of any analysis of retailing will depend to a large extent on one's success in exhibiting a typical unit in action. The intention of this section, therefore, will be to start from a static conception of store retailing with a description of its physical and functional structure, and then to pass from this to the dynamic actuality of its processes, its pace and its unceasing movement. For this purpose there has been a deliberate selection of the departmental store organisation, largely because it will afford under one roof and in a reasonably well-rounded form the most complete picture of the complexities of modern retailing. The selection will be narrowed down still further by assuming a London background and—that rare contingency—the opportunity to build an entirely new store in a carefully chosen site. Particular emphasis should be laid on this last assumption, as admittedly it contrasts with the practice of almost all British stores which are notable examples of piecemeal development.

This question of locality, once the necessary financial steps have been taken, constitutes the first fundamental problem to be tackled. Naturally the character of the neighbourhood's residential class, together with the prospects of a passing trade or of a family trade, is one dominating factor; and the physical aspects of the neighbourhood form another. The intervention, for instance, of a park or a high hill might definitely control the direction of shopping ; or a traffic terminus again might create a " pull " from some particular quarter.

A different type of factor is presented by the general strength and incidence of local competition. Our imaginary store retailer might find a concentration of the market in one or two well-defined groups ; or there might be no such demarcation, but merely a string of single shops. In either case he has to assure himself that he can act as a focal point for the area. He must do more ; he must attempt to foresee so far as he can the future possibilities of the neighbourhood. A new industrial area, for instance, such as Dagenham to-day, clearly possesses big potentialities, and equally big risks ; but in most cases, the issues are not nearly so clear cut, and the thoroughfares in and out of London are littered with derelict shopping areas that have fortuitously risen and then fallen with the popularity and decline of their surrounding neighbourhoods. The consequences of this constant shifting of residential and therefore of shopping habits give rise to a very heavy toll of wastage, and although there is no really effective method for ensuring a whole neighbourhood against such a calamity, one form of partial protection that has been freely adopted of recent years is more and more to concentrate the key shops in a well-placed market and so reinforce its drawing power. This is significant because it has in turn, of course, put a premium on sites in such strictly limited areas, and has led to a steep increase in their rentals.

The forces that govern the quality of a particular

" pitch " are in part natural, in part accidental. Obviously a corner site when available picks itself ; and the important bearing of traffic on the question can be deduced by observation.   On the other hand, the angle of sunshine and of wind do not necessarily create the popular side of the street, which frequently runs counter to them.

If, therefore, the store retailer wishes to perform his function of knitting together a shopping area, these are all prior considerations of which he must make a careful study ; and in addition he will be bearing in mind many other factors such as a good frontage for window space, and in the rear access for all incoming and outgoing vans.   Most difficult of all is the problem, not merely of picking the right site, but, where plots are staked out so close to one another, of securing, first, a large enough plot to enable a store to be built, and, secondly, scope for adjacent expansion without incurring too heavy liabilities in buying out other businesses.   This is in striking contrast to the position of the manufacturer who can ordinarily acquire at a low cost a considerable amount of spare ground to allow of the erection of further factories as and when the occasion arises.

The reconciliation of such conflicting considerations is closely related to the class of public whom the retailer hopes to serve.   The visualisation of his public is therefore of vital importance ; for on it will depend his success in anticipating and materialising their wants at prices they can afford to pay and under conditions congenial to them.   In his survey of the neighbourhood he will have ascertained the standard of merchandise and range of service already being attempted by his competitors, and also the extent to which they are effectively achieving their objective. For example, if he is interested in furniture, he may find that some one retailer has already cultivated a good-class business. Studying this man and with an eye to the normal resident purchaser, he will be able to establish the type and range of furniture which is saleable in the locality. He will next judge the size of this possible market. Then he will have to decide what are the prices that will appeal ; how far credit must be given ; how much advertising is required. Important trading issues are immediately raised by these questions, for although the virtue of a price is in the value afforded, this value is made up of a complex of factors, many of which are obscure.

There is in fact a constant pressure, not to say compulsion, on the shopkeeper—a pressure and compulsion to which he probably submits a little too faint-heartedly —to offer not merely intrinsic merchandise-value, but also certain extraneous adjuncts covered under the somewhat mystic headings of " Terms of Business " and " Service." In effect, therefore, it is the compound of all these items which goes to make up " price."

It may be well to look at it first from the point of view of the trader who enters a shopping area as a new arrival. Is he to insist right away on cash payment or is he to afford credit facilities ? It will be difficult for him not to have regard to the traditions of the neighbourhood, and he will probably find that in many directions custom can only be obtained and held by offering

the inducement of credit. This may be in the straight-
forward form of monthly accounts ; or it may be offered
through the channel of a club whereby its members are
enabled to buy goods and pay for them in instalments ;
or it may be on the direct hire-purchase system. But
whatever the form, it is clear that where accounts are
permitted, allowance must be made in a retailer's costs
for running them.

It can be left to economists to argue whether, particularly in times of depression, a social benefit does or
does not attach to schemes for buying on instalment in
order to encourage consumer-demand ; but it is illuminating to remark how far these " Terms of Business " can
draw the attention away from the essential consideration
of the real value of the purchase itself. It is a dangerous
and unhealthy state of things both for the shopkeeper
and the public when goods are not bought on their
merits, but are selected only after arrangement of financial details so delicately contrived that their real significance is hardly realised.

Accordingly the practical and inescapable points with
which the ordinary retailer is concerned at this juncture
narrow themselves down to two. On the debit side he
must make allowance for the interest on the capital
employed in financing accounts and also for the expense
incurred in their book-keeping and collection. This expense is heavy by reason of the fact that a multiplicity
of small items is involved giving rise to many hundreds
of accounts for a relatively inconsiderable turnover. On
the other hand, the second point is in their favour, seeing
that accounts can be a real facility to regular customers

and thereby consolidate such trade ; although even this can be a double-edged weapon when the store becomes bound to its customers even more than they to the store. For in this way, by too close an attention to individual peculiarities and by ministering to the whims of a long-standing clientele, enterprise can be insensibly stifled and a decline takes place, until at last a progressive newcomer has to be called in to brave the opprobrium of rescuing an old-established business from itself.

Nor is over-much credit the shopkeeper's only temptation. He will similarly require to strike a nice balance between " services " that can be termed proper to the class of business he has in view and those that go beyond this border-line. Certain of these have indeed to a large extent become necessary in the sense that their absence would definitely mean an inconvenient barrier to business. Free delivery of many types of goods might be cited as one ; and especially for food departments it constitutes quite a major item of expense which must, of course, find its place in the ultimate selling price. In many cases, too, there would be a natural expectation of lifts, and of this or that attendant at convenient spots. These again, within reason, are admissible. But it is noteworthy to-day that public wants have extended beyond the category of such " services," with the result that it is only too easy for the retailer to be diverted from his main business of merchandising and for a disproportionate attention to be devoted to writing rooms and rest rooms ; to free garage space ; or to the provision of uneconomic furnishings and trappings.

We now come to the building itself, which is to be

the instrument of the retailer's policy. To enable it to function satisfactorily as the practical and æsthetic embodiment of the store's requirements much prior study will be necessary, and the architect must at an early stage be assisted to crystallise his conception of the individual character of the business. On the practical side, he will probably postulate a rectangular building, three sides of which will provide him on the ground floor with frontage for show-windows, and the fourth at the rear with facilities for the handling of freight. The skeleton of this building he will see rising as an engineering " grid " on steel staunchions positioned so as to afford economy in cost and also to permit of flexibility in planning the interior layout. Next, within the very strict limits imposed by the Building Acts and consistent with the number and height of the storeys that have been agreed upon, he will set about securing the desired floor area and at the same time he will decide on his pivotal points, such as the public entrances, staircases and lifts.

Here then is his practical framework taking shape. But meantime, the interpretative imagination of the artist will also have been at work fashioning the elevation as a cloak to this framework, providing it with scale and proportion and adding adornment. And at every turn he will need to resolve the conflict between the practical and the æsthetic. The show-windows, for instance, constitute a whole technique of their own. They present a three-dimensional problem of size and shape which must be correctly proportioned to the needs of varying merchandise ; they demand accessibility for the

window-dresser ; and they present the store's most difficult problem in unobtrusive lighting. Further, when
taken in conjunction with the design as a whole they
very often, by reason of their measurements and in the
relation of their plate-glass expanse to structural frontage,
determine the entire scale and proportion of the elevation.

The internal planning can be conveniently considered
in three sections. The size of the building itself will to
a large extent control the allocation of space under the
first heading, which we will term architectural and engineering " losses." The size of the estimated turnover will
control the second—the selling areas ; and both size and
class of turnover the third—the non-selling areas.

Under the first heading mention has already been
made of the Building Acts which play a large part in
architectural " losses," and in London in particular
stereotype the internal disposition of a store. Ultra-
conservative fire regulations, for instance, under-prescribe
its height and over-prescribe the number of its staircases
and its means of escape. They further stipulate that
the building must be constructed in a number of water-
tight, or rather fire-tight, compartments, floor being cut
off from floor, and the staircases insulated. By these
and other means they substantially add to the costs and
incidentally prevent the attractiveness of an open layout
associated, for example, with the Parisian store.

Staircases, of course, are not the only means of circulation, and when lifts and main gangways have contributed their quota of lost footage, very probably 20
per cent. of the area available has gone in this way.
Engineering requirements will claim a further 5 per

cent. of space, so that there can be housed in the sub-
basement the plant required for heating and ventilation
and for lighting, as well as for the sprinklers which will
be installed as an insurance against fire. Altogether,
therefore, a very appreciable percentage of the total area
has to be appropriated and, in addition, heavy costs of
installation and of maintenance are involved.

Having satisfied the first and essential needs of the
building itself, the next step will be to proceed with
the general scheme for the layout of the commercial
sections of the store.

A straightforward arrangement for the architect to
adopt will be to select the heart of the building for
his second factor, the showrooms ; and then, under his
third heading to dispose appropriately around them those
non-selling activities, particularly the warehouses and
offices, which serve respectively as the main channels
of supply and of information for the selling departments.
If this customary practice is adopted, there will be placed
in either the first or second basement a whole run of
warehousing sections, concerned on the one hand with
the intake of bulk goods from the factories and on the
other hand with their subsequent packing and despatch
in retail form to the customer. It will be necessary to
keep these two flows of traffic separate, the inward flow
entailing an orderly sequence from the loading dock to
the receiving rooms where the merchandise will be in
turn unpacked, checked, examined and passed to the
reserve stock-rooms and to the selling departments ;
while the outward flow in reversing the process probably presents even more difficult problems, seeing that

it starts with a number of minor tributaries in various corners of the building. Its initial plunge may well be by means of chutes and conveyors run direct from the showrooms and converging on the despatch department in the basement. There the goods will be checked, assembled and packed. They will also be sorted for delivery in one or other of the categories employed— rail, carrier, post office or the store's own fleet of vans. With this done they can be routed for the loading dock in accordance with a time-table that must be scheduled with minute care.

This illustration will serve to indicate the size and complexity of just one of the hidden activities that is required. Both its own particular layout and its relation to the general setting need to be schemed in advance, for from the start provision will have to be made for the costly constructional work of the machinery and piping involved. Further, the theoretical example has been simplified by making the assumption that the building is a rectangle in plan and permits of straight-forward treatment. In practice this may not be the case. Indeed the actual circumstances may—on the grounds, for example, of high rental cost—even challenge the principle of handling despatch within the store proper and suggest a separate building for this and other cognate services. Moreover, the needs of the ware-housing sections will, in any case, have to be aligned with the possibly conflicting claims of other activities suitable to the basement, such as the workshops of the various trades engaged in the maintenance of the store and its equipment, or staff cloakrooms and other staff departments.

All of these activities will be allotted proportionate areas calculated on the basis of a pre-determined turnover for the store. This turnover will have been estimated as capable of practical achievement within a measurable time from the opening date, and will then have been divided and sub-divided into subsidiary totals for each of the showroom departments which it has been decided to include. It is obvious that in the application of these secondary totals the estimates here and there are bound to be considerably wide of the mark, from which it follows that the essential principle in the disposition of the selling departments will be to ensure a layout that can be inexpensively adapted to changing or over-riding circumstances. This layout therefore must be intelligible ; it must be orderly ; but above all it must be flexible. In this task there will be certain guiding considerations to assist one's judgment, and one of these will be the trading value of space, floor by floor. Quantitatively ground floor space will be expected to bulk largest, except in the case of a cheap type of trade, where the bargain basement—should an extensive one be used for selling purposes—may well prove a formidable rival. Naturally, too, as one mounts higher in the building the yield per foot will decrease, probably progressively as one advances from the first through the upper floors. Accordingly those types of merchandise which are easily carried, make a ready appeal to the casual shopper, and sell quickly, will normally be found on the ground floor. Among these are numbered the fancy and novelty departments, and perhaps perfumery, or again hose and gloves.

But a cross-current may set in with the individual history of the store—a reputation, for example, in piece-goods or in millinery, which may accordingly require allotment to this floor and a resultant displacement of some more usual department. Or, again, local tradition plays its part, such as the striking one which contrasts English practice with the German custom of placing food departments high up in the store.

The first, second and third floors will ordinarily be given over to the " family " departments, where shopping can be more leisurely and roomy. For ladies' outfitting, gowns, costumes, etc., adequate space will be wanted for display and for adjacent fitting-rooms and workrooms. For very similar reasons many of the household departments, particularly where basement space is limited, may be located on one of these upper floors. Here again at every stage adjustments will have to be made between conflicting claims, and on such matters the instinct of the merchant is of first importance. His ear must be attuned to his particular public ; he must sense the right atmosphere ; anticipate new trends and transient fashions. He cannot afford to wait on events ; he must unceasingly devise and adapt.

In this intelligent creation of demand he will be assisted by other facilities or attractions which he will be expected to offer and which he will probably place high up in the building. These may comprise a restaurant which he may attempt to run as a profit-making department in itself or merely as a necessary service ; also possibly reading- and writing-rooms, cloak-rooms, and information bureaux, which clearly cannot be expected to pay their way. Their degree of importance and their size will to a considerable extent depend on the class of customer whom he has in view, a matter which also has a very direct bearing on the extent and dimensions of the offices and counting-house. A cash trade, for example, can reduce to a minimum the heavy requirements of sales accountancy, although it may leave unaffected other aspects of statistical analysis. The grouping of all such administrative functions may well take place on the top floor, which will then be connected by tube and telephone with every other part of the business. Here, in addition to the counting-house, will be found the management, the buying offices and the advertising offices ; here, too, possibly a run of staff activities—the engagement offices, lecture rooms, the medical clinic, the recreation rooms and the canteens.

CHAPTER XII

THIS, then, in brief is the store's skeleton, its cells, organs and tissues. We now want to animate it, to set the body in motion ; and perhaps this can best be done by giving a picture of a season's work. Broadly speaking, a fresh chapter in merchandising opens before each spring season and closes with the end of the summer, while a similar span is given over to the autumn and winter trade. The years, therefore, are mapped out and punctuated with six-monthly accounts, each of them registering within their narrow limits the successes and failures of much concentrated effort.

At the nerve centre the chief executive officer—the managing director, or it may be the general manager— will be responsible for the co-ordination of all these activities ; and as it is manifestly impossible for him personally to supervise every section, he will normally devolve responsibility into five parts, each under its own manager. First and foremost comes merchandising in its dual aspect—the purchasing of goods, with its technique based largely on the impersonal appraisal of values and fashions ; and, secondly, the selling of goods, with its technique based on the personal approach to the store's typical individual customer, who is then universalised under the general heading of " the public." Next come the three main spending departments,—the staff offices, the advertising offices, and the maintenance and service departments. Finally, acting partly as servant and partly

79

as a control to all these others, we have the counting-
house.

For the adequate dovetailing of these very different
branches of activity a high degree of administrative skill
and of unbiassed judgment is required of the general
manager.   He is there to provide the oil in the machinery :
and apart from this, by reason of his position, he also
serves as the personal link between his firm and the
customer.   He must be the custodian of its good name.

How, then, does the executive plan a season's campaign ?
As the figure portion of the work will be described later,
we will for the moment assume that a sound budget has
been constructed, and that the general manager is now
in session with the merchandise manager discussing the
practical employment of the buying resources at their
disposal.   There will be a preliminary survey of the
general economic situation and of market tendencies.
This will then narrow down to decisions on the store's
merchandising policy for the season ; on certain key
projects ; on the particular allocations to be made immediately and the percentage of orders to be held temporarily in suspense as a reserve against unforeseen
contingencies.

The merchandise manager will now be ready to con-
sult individually with his team of buyers, and much will
depend upon his success in mapping out for them a
clearly defined field in which to work.   For it is his first
job to ensure that his buyers are not at sixes and sevens
among themselves and that their purchases will be conforming to a coherent and pre-arranged programme.
Within the framework of this programme they will be

furnished with certain axiomatic data. They will know, for instance, the limits of their spending power based on the anticipated turnover for the season. They will know also the salient price ranges, and the general standards of quality and of workmanship that are required. Doubtless they will further have impressed upon them by the merchandise office that the ideal at which to aim is to buy sparingly in each particular class, consistent with a reasonable assortment and with keen prices. Otherwise, the department will soon become clogged with slow-moving and therefore unprofitable stock.

Armed with this information the buyer will get in touch with the markets some three to six months before the season's opening. The work of preliminary exploration before him will be very heavy, the early stages being spent mainly in sifting out and discarding improbable tendencies and stocks until he is able to satisfy himself on a choice of significant trends. It is at this point he will find his greatest difficulty in reconciling the extensive array of likely merchandise with the strictly limited allocation that has been allowed him.

With his provisional selection made, samples must generally be submitted and examined—possibly reported on after scientific analysis—before the detailed plan of ordering can be drawn up and authorised. Its apportionment according to style, colour, size and other particulars will call for two very different qualities,—an instinctive judgment, together with statistical orderliness ; and the latter quality will again be required in abundance in scheduling the punctual delivery of the goods and then in marshalling their reception from the factories. Much

6

hurried liaison work will be needed to produce even
reasonable efficiency on these matters. Nor does the
sequence of pressure end with the routine of examination
and of ticketing bulk supplies. The stock-keepers will
determine on a physical arrangement of the merchandise
that will afford the best bird's-eye view of the current
position. They will supplement it daily and weekly with
figure checks ; and this information will then be tabu-
lated by the statistical department in such a form as to
provide a reliable gauge to the buyer for his future
ordering or " laying off." The showroom staff will
meantime have been coached on the selling qualities
of their stock, and will be bringing further first-hand
knowledge to bear upon each unit of merchandise which
is now taking on an individual character and is to be
regarded as some one customer's potential choice.

In this way the season advances interspersed with
alarums and excursions. Unexpectedly popular stocks
are caught short ; errors of judgment lead to other stocks
cumbering the shelves ; factories default or misdeliver.
But throughout the period the management is keeping a
close watch on the departmental pulse ; on the graph of
its sales by comparison with previous years ; on the graph
of its gross margin and those other elements which will
need to register satisfactorily on the ultimate balance-sheet.

Meantime everything is moving apace to the culmina-
tion of the half-year's work in the end-of-season sales,
which are designed primarily to clear the shelves of excess
merchandise and so free the warehouse for the intake of
new purchases. For idle stock means idle capital, and it is
better to realise at a loss and to reinvest rather than to

hold on to dead stock. The complete conception of a regular spring-cleaning of this kind for manufacturers, wholesalers and retailers alike has only been brought to its logical fulfilment of recent years, but it can and does play a very considerable part in the whole economy of modern retailing.

Closely allied to these merchandising activities is the advertising plan of campaign. This, too, will have been formulated in broad outline at a conference between the general manager and the advertising manager well before the season's start. First there will have been a settlement of the sum available, a figure which will naturally bear a very direct relation to the expected turn-over. There will then grow out of the firm's general line of policy a decision on the dominant themes to be employed, and this will in turn lead both to the reservation of space in suitable media and to preparatory work on catalogues and posters. By this time the advertising manager will be in a position to pursue his line of attack with the help of the buyers, who will supply him with advance information about their purchases. He will also be distributing matter to the display staff for them to co-operate in close accord. For display work, although a very recent growth, has quickly become a highly technical subject calling for more pure imagination and craftsmanship than perhaps any other branch of the store's activities ; and it is a welcome sign that already the individual character of the business can often be most successfully interpreted in the windows. It therefore not infrequently happens that, whereas the daily Press can make the best of the price, the window displays more effectively set off the appearance, and in that event there will be a slight shift in the emphasis of the appeal when passing from one to the other. But the cardinal need should be to avoid a radical divorce between the policies carried out through the various channels of publicity—newspaper, catalogue, and window. For example, a special campaign in the local or national Press which concentrated upon style and quality would very largely be nullified by a window display in which price was the dominant feature. At every turn, too, the exact synchronisation of the publicity with the selling events is of prime importance. This implies the arrangement of a carefully graduated time-table in which copy-writers, design-artists, block-makers, display workshops, window-dressers, will all play their part alongside the merchandising and selling staff : and not infrequently they will have to act as an emergency squad so as to meet the vagaries of the weather or to comply with the exacting call of some sudden demand.

The service and maintenance departments will equally be working to a very strict programme. For example, the organisation for delivering goods is comparatively large, especially where a food trade is done. Originating with the casual errand boy, who delivered the over-heavy parcel, it has now become an integral part of the business of retailing, although it is open to question whether the costs of so elaborate a system do not in some cases outrun its justification. We have already seen how in the construction of the building conveyor-belts, lifts and chutes are provided for the conveyance of goods from the show-rooms to the despatch department in the basement. There the checking, sorting and routing will have in view carefully delineated areas and a rigorous time-table in which the long-distance vans will leave for the country districts early in the morning, while the nearer neighbourhoods will be served at more frequent intervals throughout the day. It will be obvious that parcels for some districts cannot be accepted after a certain hour,— a factor which will require constant adjustment between customer, sales-person and packer.

Maintenance is similarly a matter of daily routine, and the store's superintendent will be in control of quite a small army of engineers, carpenters, electricians, porters, cleaners and charwomen. In addition to seeing to the good repair of the building inside and out, they will also supply from their own workshops all the temporary and some of the permanent fixtures and equipment which are required from time to time.

Perhaps this department can provide the best picture of the diversity and magnitude of the store's organisation. Two floors below the surface there will be found compactly assembled, generators producing light and power ; refrigerating plant, heating and cooling plant, devices for cleansing the air, and most of those engineering intricacies which are usually associated with the bowels of a ship, together with others fulfilling the store's special needs.

It will be immediately apparent from the preceding pages that the staff manager is faced with a range of interesting problems. He will be concerned with the engagement of personnel covering pretty well the whole industrial gamut of age, aptitudes and calibre, with a widely varying background of education and experience.

On most occasions he will be selecting for an individual job and with an eye to the idiosyncrasies of a particular supervisor. The set mental or mechanical test, therefore, will be applicable in only a limited number of cases, and will probably merely act as a groundwork in sorting out the more junior staff. His major need will be good judgment, partly intuitive, partly experienced, in assessing character and ability.

Once the applicant has been selected, one of the primary aims of the staff manager must be to assist him in achieving a corporate outlook. The diversity of the personal material and the sectionalisation of the work are both obstacles to overcome, and make it very necessary to seize on every opportunity for impressing the store's rules and policy on the staff by individual word of mouth, by precept, by lectures and discussions. In addition, more technical training in merchandise and in systems has to be afforded. This is a recurrent problem ; and courses arranged inside the store can be supplemented with others obtainable outside.

A natural corollary to this work will be his concern with matters of health, welfare and recreation ; and there may also be imposed on him yet a further duty of assessing and allotting the sales-force quota to each department. Based on previous experience and on standard performances, there will be an agreed percentage,—probably varying departmentally,—allowed to each for wages ; and once the firm's estimated budget of sales has been fixed for the half-year, the staff manager will arrange with the departments that this percentage is adhered to.

In point of numbers, the allocation will have to bear in

mind each category of graduated experience from senior hands down to juniors, and to make provision for a sufficiency to carry on in the slack periods (on the war-time parallel of a safe minimum of troops for every mile of front-line trench). These will receive further help from an emergency squad in times of exceptional pressure. In point of expenditure, the counting of " heads " will then have to be converted at their varying rates into £ s. d. results, and a margin left for the provision of temporary staff, commission payments, and other contingencies. Finally, the total of all these, by virtue of the most careful manipulation, will have to conform to the prescribed allowance ; and the same general process will need to be applied to all the non-selling sections as well as to the showrooms themselves.

Treasury contact with other branches of the business comes out clearly and immediately on this point, and it is an aspect which will be further developed in the next chapters under the heading of Budgetary Control. Meantime we are more concerned with accountancy pure and simple, whereby the counting-house, in dealing with the cash, with the ledgers, and with statistical analysis, acts as the servant of others. The handling of cash presents three normal alternatives—an allotment of cashiers to each department, a centralised installation connected through a network of tubes with the show-rooms, or, in quick-change departments, an arrangement for small groups of assistants to run their own cash register tills.

On the bought ledger side, a strictly limited staff will be entering and settling purchases and expenses. The technique of this portion of the accountancy entails for each transaction contact between two business houses, both of them conforming to a known system, and is therefore comparatively simple and regular.

By way of contrast this throws into relief the intricacy and multiplicity of the sales ledgers with their resultant large staffs. The opening of each individual account is discretionary ; the items to be charged are generally small ; the process of collection is, in the first place, dependent on the customer's active goodwill or good manners, and at a later stage, should it arise, creates much extra expense and trouble. However satisfactory a technique is evolved, therefore, the whole procedure is always liable to become unduly wasteful.

For different reasons the multiplicity of small items also makes the routine of statistical analysis an unsatisfactory, because tedious, job. This material is compiled from the duplicates of the sales-dockets which every day are sent through to the clerks in the dissecting room for checking and extraction. The information on these dockets relates not only to the individual assistant and the section concerned, but also to the type of sale and category of merchandise. It is necessary to build up these records daily in order to serve as an immediate pointer to departmental trends : but more valuable still are their cumulative totals which from month to month and season to season go to form the basis of budgetary control.

CHAPTER XIII

BUDGETARY CONTROL OF MERCHANDISING

BROADLY speaking, there are two well-defined aspects of retailing—the stock or merchandising aspect, which concerns itself with the purchase of the right categories and quantities of goods for sale at the right time; and the administrative aspect, which concerns itself with the efficiency and economy of the general organisation, so as to ensure as far as possible that it ends up with a profit at the end of the year. There are similarly two natural divisions of budgetary control that follow suit. These can be most easily explained if we work backwards.

The final objective for the trader is, of course, to secure a percentage of nett profit which will remunerate him for his investment of money and labour. He knows by experience that in order to achieve a given amount of turnover upon which this nett profit must ultimately depend, he must incur a certain minimum total of expenses by way of wages, rent, and so on, which can be broadly assessed from year to year as a percentage ratio to turnover. He has, therefore, over the store as a whole, to price his goods so as to provide a sufficiency both for these on-costs or expenses, and for his residual nett profit.

The control of his expenses is termed in this and the succeeding chapter the administrative side of budgetary control; but it will at once be seen that it is only a control within a larger framework. The framework itself consists of his merchandising policy, which in turn possesses two aspects,—quantitative, i.e. bulk sales ; qualitative, i.e. profitable sales. Merchandising control is concerned with the parallel attainment of these two goals ; and their joint product furnishes the margin (called gross margin) out of which expenses and nett profit can be met.

To take a perfectly simple example, we might start with a shop capable of doing £10,000 worth of business. We equip it and staff it to achieve that figure, and then estimate that the total of expenses, together with a modicum of nett profit, will with economical handling require £2500. Our problem, then, is so to merchandise that we succeed in getting our turnover of £10,000 on the basis of selling for that figure goods which have cost us at their point of bulk reception not more than £7500.

How, then—to continue the process of working backwards—do we set about ensuring that this needed margin of £2500 will be made available ? In our example the limit is patently set at one end with the known factor of goods costing £7500 ; but the unknown element comes at the other end, which is dependent upon our degree of success in selling the goods profitably all the way along the line. If we could be sure that the stock which has cost £7500 would, in fact, sell for £10,000, the merchandising problem would be simple, as we could then add to the cost price of each article a sufficient percentage to bring the aggregate sales at the end of the year to approximately £10,000 : but in practice it does not work out in this way. Buying mistakes are inevitable, and it is certain that some portion of the stock that has been acquired will not sell at the prices originally anticipated. Thus, with our example of goods costing £7500 it may well be that the realised turnover of £10,000 will actually be made up—

(a) of the bulk which, costing £6500, sell roughly in accordance with anticipation at £9000 ;

(b) of the residue which, costing £1000, have eventually to be cleared after much effort at no more than their cost figure.

In the initial instance, of course, each range of merchandise is priced or " marked up " to yield its proper margin, so that the total of the priced values at the start may reach, say, £10,500. But at the same time it is known from previous experience that on an average expectation the goods are not likely to fetch more than about £10,000 in all. Mark-up, therefore, has consistently in view the practical necessity for subsequent reductions on certain portions of the stock, on which a sale can only be effected at a sacrifice.

We can now put the various stages of the process in their proper order :—

(a) First we have the cost price taken from the purchase invoices, together with sundry stock charges.

(b) To this will be added a percentage called the " initial mark-up."

(c) Mark-up is a hypothetical figure ; and in actual fact is, as we have seen, subject to certain wastages. It must therefore be high enough, after allowing for all such mistakes, and for both known and unknown losses, to leave a predetermined percentage of " Gross Margin."

(d) This percentage of gross margin must, in turn, be sufficient to meet expenses and to leave a residual nett profit.

As the technicalities of pricing are generally so little known, it may be helpful to give briefly some further information under the headings just mentioned :—

Cost Price.—It should at once be noted that the amounts paid to factories and warehouses for incoming merchandise do not constitute the sole purchase charge. There may also be attendant costs entailed prior to, or in the course of bringing the goods to the door of the store, such as any charges for buyers' travelling, for insurance and the inward transportation of the goods. Next, when the merchandise actually has been delivered, further charges may arise from time to time in repairing or making good damaged stock. These are sometimes termed Stock Expenses.

Again, charges arise with another category of incoming merchandise made in the store's own productive departments, such as the dressmaking workrooms and cabinet workshops. Some of these should be classed as "service" departments, in that they are run as necessary adjuncts to the selling departments, even although, judged strictly on their own merits, they may not pay their way. As an instance of this, one may cite alteration workrooms in connection with ready-to-wear departments ; carpet planners and layers in connection with carpet and linoleum departments ; and polishers, solely employed for the purpose of touching up and putting in good condition any furniture sold by the retail departments. These examples will explain how stock charges arise over and above the actual purchase price of merchandise.

Initial Mark-Up.—When buying, a buyer sees his cost price in relation to a presumed selling price ; and the latter has to satisfy in his mind two not necessarily compatible tests.   In anticipation, it must aim at being strictly competitive in value, while in present fact it must also be able to bear such a rate of initial mark-up as will enable him, after making due allowance for contingencies, to achieve the rate of gross margin required from his department by the management.

These tests, of course, cannot be applied literally to each individual unit of purchase, but groups of selling ranges should produce in average the desired result.

This then is the operation known as the " Initial Mark-Up."   The resultant selling price marked on the ticket represents nothing more than the figure which the buyer hopes the article will realise.   From the start, however, he knows that over the whole range of his goods certain factors are bound to arise which will make considerable inroads into this margin of mark-up, and it is these factors of allowances, losses and depreciation which bring about in actual practice a scaling down from the level of the initial mark-up to the lower and final level represented by the gross margin actually earned on the merchandise that is sold.   In fact, the gap between these two levels probably accounts in all for an unseen loss that varies between 5 and $7\frac{1}{2}$ per cent., according to the category of the merchandise ; and precisely because it is unseen by the outside public, it is for that reason very little understood by them, and, indeed, not adequately appreciated by the majority of retailers themselves.

Mark-Downs, etc.—The commonest and largest cause for this gap arises from a depreciation in value necessitating " Mark-Downs " of stock.   Any miscalculations

in buying, either of kind or quantity ; any lack of pre-
vision as to possible changes of fashion ; any mistake as
to wearing qualities ; misfits ; an ill-assortment of sizes
or colours or shapes ; a failure in time,—any or all of
these causes give rise to a logical chain of events, for which
the final account is only rendered when reductions take
effect at the half-yearly sales, or at the annual re-valuation
of stocks.   Furthermore, these half-yearly sales have now
become such an important feature of retailing that at
such times bulk stocks throughout the store are normally
offered at a discount, irrespective of the factors mentioned,
and solely on the ground that sale-time is discount-time.
It is, in effect, an attempt to achieve volume at an otherwise dead end of the season on a deliberately lower level
of gross margin.

In the showrooms similar and further possibilities of
loss occur—perhaps a lack of liaison in affording the
merchandise an adequate display ; in some cases physical
damage or soiling of stock ; in others a customer's dis-
satisfaction, giving rise to an allowance or replacement.

Then there is a not inconsiderable category of un-
detected deficiencies which come to light only at the
periodic stocktakings.   Physical shortages may arise,
for example, in piece-goods departments as the result of
small over-measurements or odd lengths, or the provision
of patterns ; in food departments as wastage ; and in all
departments by reason of error, or even dishonesty,
either on the part of the public or of the staff.

Gross Margin is an expression less commonly employed
than gross profit ; but the latter is undoubtedly misleading
in that its immediate implication to the layman is that

at most a relatively minor agenting charge has to be met out of it by the retailer, and that the major portion of his excess over manufacturing price is accordingly sheer profit. Put in the simplest terms and stripped of the technicalities arising out of the overlapping factor of opening and closing stocks, a retailer's gross margin is the total difference between the purchase price of incoming merchandise (inclusive of any attendant costs involved) and the amount actually realised by the sale of this same merchandise after deducting the various allowances, losses and depreciation which, as we have already seen, inevitably arise.

It will be appreciated, therefore, that these " mark-downs " and other losses become an exceedingly important factor. Firstly, they must be accurately assessed so that adequate provision can be made for them in the " initial mark-up." Secondly, they must be rigorously controlled, because if they are allowed to get out of hand, they will reduce the gross margin—from which, as has been explained, expenses and nett profit have to come—to a dangerously low level. This also serves to emphasise the vital importance of correctly determining the percentage of gross margin to be aimed at. It must not be set so high that the resultant selling prices are not competitive with those of other retailers catering for the same class of customer. On the other hand, it must not be so low that it cannot meet the expenses entailed in securing the desired turnover.

Gross margin, therefore, becomes the first of the retailer's objectives for the year based on the assumption that he can keep his second objective, his total of expenses, within the limits he has thus set himself. Accordingly, the practical merchandising problem before him is so to control his losses on mark-up as to ensure the maintenance of the desired gross margin.

With this end in view we are now ready to consider the steps taken in a departmental store to install effective merchandise control. It will have been seen that the two key factors on which depends the whole budgetary control of the store's merchandising activities are (1) Turnover; and (2) Gross Margin. Turnover will be the first and over-riding consideration, and the initial problem will therefore be to forecast the year's trade with reasonable accuracy. There then immediately follows the classification of this estimated turnover under its departmental heads so as to furnish the basis for sanctioning stock purchases. Each departmental division and subdivision requires a separate analysis from several angles, but all of them are severally and jointly concentrated on the one ultimate objective of securing by the year's end the correct gross margin.

This can only be done if the retailer succeeds in keeping his stocks constantly on the move, or " turning over," to use the more technical term. If he fails in this, it will mean that his shelves will become loaded with unwanted and unseasonable goods, and he will inevitably find that he is exceeding his allowance for mark-downs. Apart therefore from any flair for his job which he may possess, it is important that he should be guided and assisted by certain simple statistical records. These records, in the first place, will provide him with his periodic limits for buying, so that he can accurately dispose of his orders according to the seasonal fluctuations. For this purpose the year can be split up into weeks or months, as is the case, for example, with clothing departments, or into weeks and even days in the case of food departments.

Other sets of figures may be furnished to indicate the correct apportionment of stock according to types, and styles, and price ranges ; possibly also according to fittings, sizes and colours. Everything, in fact, will be done to break up the aggregate totals into smaller units, so as to facilitate the intelligent handling of his merchandise and to encourage closer control.

The building-up of this control is, in the first place, empirical. Let us presuppose that rule-of-thumb methods have failed and the task ahead of us is to formulate departmental standards, using at all possible turns the buyer's specific and intuitive experience, but cross-checking it where we can by a more general sense of proportion and statistical practice. Each department will present a different set of ingredients, every one of which requires its proper weighting before it is possible to settle the optimum stock level—a level that should in any case rise or fall in partial accord with the monthly graph of business. There are extraneous circumstances to take into account, such as the traditions of the particular trade. It may be that factory requirements will encourage the purchase of goods some months ahead, or in considerable bulk, so as to get the benefit of discounts based on quantity. This will present a stiffer stock problem than merchandise which can be speedily replenished from the warehouses in small lots and at frequent intervals, and it is a question of setting off the advantage against the compensating disadvantage. There is also the curve of the season's trade to consider, particularly where the possibilities are limited to a few short weeks—a type that might be termed the " now or never " purchase.

Internally, the pull of conflicting factors is equally intriguing. Wherever fashion plays a predominant part, as, for instance, with millinery, it is essential to keep the merchandise constantly changing and up-to-date, with the result that the stock-turn for this department is almost uniformly higher than for any other. And yet despite this movement, so serious is the element of depreciation by the season's close, that the loss on mark-down can be of considerable moment in its final showing. At the opposite end a reputation may have been acquired through offering a very comprehensive range and assortment in, say, piece-goods, or perhaps in men's clothing and foot-wear, where there is a strong bias towards staple, and therefore less hazardous, articles. This will give rise to a slow if steady stock-turn, but the risks of bad stock are considerably limited by the factor of constancy.

At every stage, therefore, a balance has to be struck between opposing dictates, but inevitably the final criteria should be, first, the amount of capital employed in stocks, in equipment and in space (for space possesses a capitalisation value equally with the others that are more physically obvious) ; secondly, the ratio of this capital to the trade done ; and, thirdly, the " quality " of the trade expressed concretely in terms of gross margin. As we have seen, the most vital connecting-link between these three is the control of stock-turn.

Nor should it be forgotten that this control has to be

operated while the machine is in unceasing motion.   It is true that the budget has been constructed in advance by the management for a six-months' campaign, and that this has been further classified into time-stages and allocated in departmental proportions.   The merchandise offices and the buyers have then followed suit with detailed provisions for their needs.   But as the season advances an unremitting grip is required to meet unforeseen contingencies ;   to repair omissions and misjudgments ;   and to scour the markets afresh, so that the reserve of orders, which has generally been held in hand, can be placed to take advantage of mid-season offers or unexpected developments.   Accordingly, a budget will perhaps be scrapped, reconstructed and scrapped afresh in the light of current happenings ;   for the whole technique of control, while soundly principled in conception, must be opportunist in action.   Otherwise it will merely register a series of burials.

The basis for retail pricing is the percentage system ; and at this stage it may be as well to stress the implications of this principle.   Roughly, according to the class and type of trade, there will be a standard performance for expenses, and this performance is expressed as a percentage of turnover.   This, in turn, gives rise to a standard percentage of gross margin to be aimed at.   The buyer will be armed with this knowledge, and will then adopt exactly the same practice in marking-up his goods, i.e. bearing in mind the desired gross margin, he will make a percentage addition * to his cost prices sufficient for this

* *Note.*—As all percentages are calculated in relation to selling prices, the mark-up addition is in its actual result converted into a percentage *off* the selling price, so as to bring it into line with other figures.

purpose. In effect, this means that there always exists a very constant ratio between purchase price and selling price. Accordingly, a department which to-day buys at, say, an average of 20s. per unit, to sell at an average 30s. (the mark-up in this instance representing a hypothetical 33⅓ per cent.) would, with a change of purchase price to 22s., sell at 33s., or vice versa, with a change to 18s. sell at 27s. It should be emphasised that this is practically the automatic result of any widespread movement upwards or downwards in the average price level of its purchases, the underlying theory being that its operative costs should vary about proportionately with the fluctuations of its purchase prices, so that in the simple example quoted, distributive expenses on a rising market have to be met out of 11s. ; on a normal market out of 10s. ; on a falling market out of 9s.

Naturally, there are one or two qualifications, such as the time-lag, which temporarily delays the rapidity of the rise or fall by reason of prior stocks that have to be worked off ; and the factor of averaging which also smoothes out the steeper seasonal and other curves. But, taken by and large, the practice has been accepted almost as an axiom, and with very little conscious attention to its partial fallibility in certain sets of circumstances. This has peculiar significance in to-day's conditions, firstly because in many directions the purchase prices to the retailer have been consistently falling for over ten years, and secondly because in an era of increasing mass-production there is considerable likelihood, if a long-range view is taken, of a continued drop in factory prices over important ranges of goods. It is therefore possible to visualise the day when the general theory of an unvarying percentage addition to cost price will be in danger of breaking down, for where expenses remain stationary in £. s. d. outlay, they obviously increase as a percentage burden at a time when the levels of cost prices, gross margin and selling prices are all on the down-grade.

Unfortunately, very few authoritative records are available to throw further light on recent trends. Systems of figure control such as will permit of detailed comparison have only been installed in quite recent years, even among progressive firms, but certain valuable data have been obtained which show :—

1. That approximately during the years 1914-20 total expenses rose as a percentage burden in relation to turnover, and that gross margin just kept pace with this increase so as to afford a very constant percentage of net profit throughout the period. As might be expected, the most noticeable increase in the expenses was inside the wage account.

2. That in the succeeding decade the percentage total for expenses has been held remarkably steady, thus evidencing in particular the salutary results of the unremitting control which has been exercised in post-war trading, as this period has witnessed on a wide scale the immediately effective introduction of budgetary planning. Without the assistance of this new technique there is no doubt that the burden of expenses would have mounted much higher at a time when prices have been consistently falling. Even as it is, it has naturally been impossible to prevent a rise in certain accounts, as, for example, rates, while wages have probably also been a generally heavier charge. But

these increases have been offset by rigorous economies in other directions. The corollary of this pegging down of expenses is to be found in the parallel consistency of the percentages for both gross margin and net profit. Indeed, it is worth yet further emphasis that where before there was a well-established practice and an almost ingrained habit for retailers to work on traditional percentage lines for certain elementary matters such as mark-up and the expenses total, this practice is now being fortified and keyed up by the detailed figure control which is concerned with achieving consciously planned records in every direction. Once achieved, the record becomes a standard performance for succeeding years. In an era, therefore, of falling prices the percentage basis acts as a most effective spur to the trader and safeguard for the public.

CHAPTER XIV

BUDGETARY CONTROL OF EXPENSES

HAVING explained the methods employed to secure the proper rate of gross margin, it is now possible to turn to the second stage of budgetary control involving a study of the administrative side, which is concerned with the expenses or " overheads " of the business, and with the resultant nett profit. Here again it is a pity that the term " Overheads " has been taken over from manufacturing accountancy, and has been somewhat misapplied to retailing. Speaking broadly, the factory in turning out a manufactured article changes the aspect of the raw material employed in such a way that the work done and the value created is clear to the simplest intelligence because a physical transformation has been effected. The public, therefore, accepts the costs involved in the transformation, and these ordinarily include the complete running of the factory as well as the actual process of manufacturing. Naturally, therefore, these costs easily overshadow in magnitude the few " Overheads " which remain to be added as being necessary for the sale of the final product in bulk quantities.

On the other hand, the retailer's " Overheads " constitute his most important problem of costs, and the term should not be allowed to obscure the fact that by the very nature of his business it is precisely these expenses which are for the most part the equivalent of a manufacturer's productive costs, his act of " transformation " entailing in each separate sale the adjustment of a multiplicity of factors to an individual requirement.

Further, whereas the product of machine-power can be multiplied, and therefore cheapened in striking degree, the physical limit of man-power is soon reached, and in the main, of course, distribution is and must remain largely dependent on man-power. It follows, therefore, that with every advance in the technique and scale of mass-production the essence of retailing procedure becomes more and more a matter of halving and re-halving, of quartering and re-quartering, and a breaking down and re-distribution of mass-articles into still finer sub-divisions. These processes entail labour and consequential costs that by comparison look extravagantly high.

It is important, therefore, to bear constantly in mind that the legitimate value of an article at the point at which it reaches the public is not merely the cost of the finished product in bulk, but this prime cost plus a further distributive " on-cost " in respect of a series of marketing processes and services—services of selection, disposition, presentation and finally of distribution in single and, if taken separately, often negligible units. To this end the markets of the world are scoured, the merchandise brought together and focussed in convenient shopping districts, and finally delivery effected to the doors of the public.

Budgetary control is concerned with efficiency in selling as well as economy in selling. With this in view the retailer possesses three main selling " instruments," all of which he can employ in varying degrees and proportions in his efforts to win business. He will require personnel to effect the sale ; a place in which to sell ; and possibly also other media through which to make known his wares. It will be useful to follow through with this tripartite classification as these " instruments " naturally find their counterparts in three main avenues of expenditure. First in point of time, as well as of importance, is the human " instrument," the Employment factor. This in reality forms a very comprehensive group, seeing that a sale only becomes effective when a number of individuals have co-ordinated in the sequence of its execution. It entails, for instance, staff activities of buying, warehousing, publicity, display and selling, together with maintenance, accountancy and in many cases delivery as well.

The second " instrument " of selling is the factor of the building, its occupancy, its equipment and its upkeep ; and the costs of this group are often classed under the general heading of Occupancy. Probably only within the last generation or so has the retailer become generally conscious of the potentialities that lie to hand here, a fact which may help to explain his somewhat faltering and often misapplied approach to this question. But the underlying conception should be that time and thought spent on making the building express the functional individuality of the business are well spent, when they ensure that the appropriate architecture of the shop front and the orderly layout of the interior, together with the attraction of its equipment, become real adjuncts to salesmanship.

Similarly with the third " instrument," the still younger growth of Publicity. By word and by picture, advertisements and displays act as sign-posts, provide information, furnish a running commentary, tabulate and announce the season's products or the week's latest values.

The " rightful economy " of distribution, therefore, consists in the effective and concerted employment of all these " instruments." But the complete conception is a comparatively modern one, with the result that instances of mis-, over- and under-employment can be frequently seen ; and the public's varying reactions to such mis-uses may well have a considerable bearing on the future curve of the expense ratio. A further analysis of each group of charges may therefore be advisable at this stage.

Wages Expense

In a departmental store or multiple shop the salary and wage expense (the employment factor) probably accounts for a full half of the total overheads, and therefore uses up nearly a half of the gross margin. If, therefore, we take somewhat arbitrarily the normal range of the latter as falling within the percentage limits of 20 to 30 (i.e. where the average selling-price index is a 100, the retailer's average cost price may be anything from 70 to 80, the variation, as we have already seen, being dependent chiefly upon the quality of the trade and the category of mer-chandise), then the employment charge is probably repre-sented by the range 10 to 14 per cent.*

Seeing that this expenditure stands out from all others as far and away the largest, it is obvious that budgetary control must, in the first place, be concentrated on the

* These figures and others that follow are probably more reliable pointers in the case of the stores operating mostly in clothing and furnishings. The food group of departments will show striking variations from the above, many of them being operated on less than 20 per cent. gross margin.

employment roll as being easily the most vital factor ; and a sectional analysis of all the wage items has to be carried out. Speaking broadly, it is probable that the following simple table represents the normal allocation of this expenditure, where the total employment percentage is 10 :

		Per cent.
1. Buying staff	2	7*
2. Selling staff, including a small allowance for delivery	5	
3. Administrative staff, counting-house, publicity and maintenance staffs, etc.	3	
Total wage roll	10	

A full two-thirds of the total wage costs, therefore, is closely concerned with merchandising proper. The first category, buying, carries a small number of highly important staff,—merchandise managers, buyers and their respective assistants ; and these are supported by the warehouse staff, who are responsible for the reception, marking off and storage of the goods. Certain notable social tendencies, such as the quickening of pace and variety of fashion, the products of an age of invention, and the greater accessibility of foreign markets arising out of the development of transport, have been adding considerably to the intricacy of this work.

These same tendencies similarly condition much of the work of the second category, the selling staff ; and it is probably only necessary to mention a department or two at random to bring instant recognition of the revolution that has been, and is still, taking place. The raw materials and buying processes that are now invoked in

* The delivery expense for food departments is, however, of course by no means an inconsiderable item.

the manufacture of hose have, for instance, changed the face of things in the showrooms ; and perhaps in an even more striking way the shoe department is undergoing a two-fold invasion, the one parallel to the development of fashion in hose, and the other a sterner and not necessarily compatible problem, the problem of foot anatomy and of more scientific shoe-fitting.   It follows, therefore, that salesmanship for these assistants no longer remains a job of memorising and drawing on a strictly limited stock of staple articles.   There is now brought into far greater prominence the need for a very real knowledge of the varied uses and limitations of the merchandise handled.

The allowance for selling wages, besides being the largest individual total in the employment group, also naturally constitutes as between departments the most variable factor, seeing that it is very directly dependent upon the kind of merchandise to be sold.   It therefore requires departmental, and even sectional, analysis at very frequent intervals.   The governing factor in its size is probably the habits of the shopping public ; for staff has to be carried to meet the seasonal " peak " periods of pressure.   The full implications of this statement may not at first sight be apparent, so that it is well to add the explanation that there are not only seasonal times of pressure which bear upon this problem, but, in addition, certain days of pressure in the week, and certain hours in the day increase the difficulties with which the sales-force has to cope.   Conversely, the slack periods, slack days, slack hours present the problem of a standing charge of considerable moment.   This experience of an " idle " sales-force is repeated in other directions.   For instance, the area of the building itself is governed by the demands to be made on it in heavy times, when the full tide of customers has to be served in the showrooms, and the offices and despatch departments are fully manned. This means that if all the slack hours are added up, expensive space is lying idle or semi-idle for a considerable proportion of the year. The position is, of course, in direct contrast to that of a factory planned to take a steady output, with possibly even two regular shifts a day.

An interesting parallel, on the other hand, and one that perhaps it is easier to recognise because it meets the eye so frequently, is the post-war development of transport in large cities, where the public, even in the slack middle hours of the day do not take kindly to any considerable curtailment of the services. The organisation apparently has to be based upon the regular two-minute, or it may be five-minute, supply of bus, tram and tube, even though the stream of bus, tram and tube is far more empty than full. Incidentally, so far as London is concerned, the citation of this parallel also brings to light an example of the interesting conflict of requirements that can arise between different undertakings ; for whereas the transport companies do everything they can to encourage by means of cheap tickets travelling inside the hours of 10 a.m. and 4 p.m., the stores would be benefited in expense by the more even distribution of shopping over a full run of hours from 9 a.m. to 6 p.m., more particularly as their sales-force is bound to be seriously depleted round about mid-day, even although staff lunches may be taken in three shifts.

It is, of course, admittedly the responsibility of the

management to devise means of alleviation. In busy periods an emergency staff can be used to a limited degree to assist hard-pressed departments, and overtime —also to a limited degree—can be worked. In slack periods, training and other work is carried on.

Nevertheless, the fact remains that shopping habits can, and do, lend an unconscious but undoubtedly expensive seal of approval to the well-worn line : " They also serve who only stand and wait."

The third category of wage expense quoted above is more of an omnibus character, and almost inevitably the severest eye is turned on this portion of the appropriation which accounts for the final 30 per cent. of the full wage roll. The selling staffs constitute the front-line trenches, and while they alternate between standing and waiting, and running and serving, category 3 (for the most part) sits and works. Its control is none the easier for that ; and here again modern trends of consumer demand are adding to the complications. If, for instance, the controller of expense turns to the counting-house, he will almost certainly find a definite increase in the number of customers desiring credit facilities—a tendency the costs of which he may have been fortunate enough for a time to offset by a speeding up of his organisation with the use of accountancy machines ; but which, if it continues, will in the long run lead to a larger overhead. In the neighbouring dissecting room the problems will be accumulating in direct proportion to the growing multiplicity of merchandising units. If he examines the publicity and display staff, he will find them small in numbers but headed by a few highly skilled and highly remunerated people engaged in developing a new technique. The maintenance staff of engineers, carpenters, electricians, lift-men, cleaners and night-watchmen also add their quota ; and granted the equipment they are there to maintain, the possibilities then limit themselves to a rigid control of a predetermined expense. Finally, the category includes the executive staff, working at the nerve centre and concerned with the co-ordination of one and all of these growing intricacies and activities.

At every stage, therefore, the budget for employment expense in any individual store that is well conducted throws out very little hope for large specific savings in the numbers employed, for the control is unceasing, and the total figures are constantly related to the predetermined percentage that has been allowed. There is this further complication, that selling areas must be staffed and services maintained continuously, so that when in times of adverse trade the store has scaled down to the safety level for staff, nothing more can wisely be done. Yet a further avenue of economy is thus closed to the retailer, for whereas factories are able in many cases to exercise a considerable measure of control by shutting down for holidays, working at half-pressure, and generally manipulating their hours to the needs of their output, none of these measures is available to the distributive trades, which, as servants of the public, must remain open all the time.

But a study of this question would not be complete without touching on certain more general considerations that are bound to come up for periodic review by retailing associations—questions such as the type and sex of the staffs employed, rates of pay, hours and other conditions of work. These considerations are largely inter-related, and it is, of course, only possible to speak with authority of the better organised portions of the trades, but in their case at any rate it is of significance to note that there was certainly no marked, if any, falling off in the level of wages paid during the decade 1920 to 1930, which furnished a steady decline in retailing prices. This is particularly pertinent support for the claim that has been advanced that expenses are not decreasing. The pay, however, together with the hours and status of the distributive employee in pre-war days was comparatively poor. There was, therefore, considerable leeway to make up, and a comparison with pre-war rates is not necessarily apposite. So far as can be gauged, the standards of pay to-day may very possibly be in the neighbourhood of 100 per cent. on the average over 1914. Two points are worthy of note. Firstly, in the largest centres, such as London, it is not always easy, despite the improved status of distributive staffs, to secure the right type of young trainees as sales-people, because parents and teachers favour for their brighter pupils the safer and more sheltered conditions of banks, insurance companies and professional offices. Secondly, as with other trades, the greatest advances in pay have gone to the unskilled or semi-skilled sections, such as drivers, porters, cleaners, etc., who probably average fully 120 per cent. over their pre-war standards.

Another factor that is not without importance has been the comparative absence of " casualisation " in distribution. It has already been shown that there is a considerable ebb and flow in the weekly and seasonal volume of business, but despite this it has been the general rule, on the grounds of the skill of the work required, for an adequate staff to be maintained and given continuity of employment. This arrangement possesses advantages to the community as well as to the retailer in that it promotes efficiency and self-respect all round, and is in contra-distinction to the practice of certain manufacturing industries which for some years past have operated on the principle of employing " casual " labour that is main-tained for the rest of the week by unemployment benefit.

It should, therefore, be borne in mind that an in-dividual trade's operating costs can be artificially reduced, but it is at the expense of the rest of the community. Hitherto, the distributive trades have for the most part carried their main staffs right through the slack seasons as well as the busy ones, and have also had in effect to provide in their costs for a subsidy to other industries who have either been unable or unwilling to do the same.

Occupancy Expense

The second group of expenditure to be considered is conveniently classed under the heading of Occupancy ; and for the purposes of this enquiry may be held to cover broadly rent and rates ; interest on capital employed in equipment, lighting and heating ; upkeep of the building ; upkeep of equipment ; and depreciation. As a type of expenditure it differs fundamentally from all others in that its bulk cost is determined in advance for a term of years. This applies whether a building is erected by the owner-occupier, in which case an equivalent allowance to rent has in effect to be made in the shape of the interest that is chargeable on the capital employed in this way and equally on the accompanying plant and equipment; or whether a lease of premises is taken involving an ordinary rental charge in the accounts.

Naturally, the business acumen and judgment required for this prior evaluation of a long-term development may be very different from qualities that will prove successful in the daily trading activities of distribution; and once the position has been sized up and the commitments entered into, there is very little room for further control of this type of expenditure. Pre-eminently, therefore, the charge for rent, etc., is static, and *ipso facto* it is becoming to-day an increasing percentage burden as prices fall. Equally, of course, it has to be admitted that where these commitments were fixed in pre-war days on the basis of pre-war values, the lessees have benefited considerably for the last decade; but the point to remember is that as buildings get replaced or leases become renewable, this adventitious circumstance ceases to apply. Indeed, it is safe to say that many firms reputed to be making a moderate or even striking success to-day, do so as much because of their artificially low rental charge as because of legitimate trading profits. This cannot continue indefinitely.

At the crucial stage, then, when new premises become obligatory, what are the conditions that the individual retailer experiences, and how far can he induce by his foresight a favourable rental showing for the future? More and more he will find a concentration of traders upon well-defined centres, and a scarcity value attached to such "pitches." The concentration may or may not prove a very real boon and convenience to the public, but as with the question of shopping hours, the relevant issue is the evident fact of a definite shopping habit, and to stay out of the centres is in most cases to court trouble. Further, it is well known in the property market that the stringency is increased by the policy of the Banks, who all too frequently compete for corner sites, with a consequential raising of values in their adjacent neighbourhoods. (It has indeed been satirically observed in another connection that the downfall of England dates from the time when public-houses were content to cede to the Banks their prescriptive rights over corner positions.)

The pace once set in this way, the individual trader has little option in the matter, especially when the multiple retailers vie eagerly with one another for the available sites and in this one direction, at any rate, are apparently prepared to support an inflated market value. A conservative outlook, however, is bound to view this striking tendency with disquietude ; nor does the burden cease with rent, as a consequential rise in rateable values follows suit, thus entailing a further load on the occupancy charge.

It should further be remembered that although, when a store trader enters into a lease, he is committed immediately to a minimum run of known obligations, it by no means follows that this minimum also becomes a maximum. Should he make a success of the venture, he will by his efforts have created a market for the surrounding property ; but he will not be allowed to benefit by the increment, even in the case of his own property. On the contrary, he will suffer from it, for his rateable value will go up against him and this in turn will give rise, for instance, to an increased assessment for water rate, even although his usage of the latter does not alter in any respect. After a period of years, therefore, it is even possible for this example of the water rate to be doubled as a charge. Later on, too, when he comes to a renewal of his lease, he will again be faced with the penalty of his own endeavours and will be required to pay an enhanced rent. To some extent, of course, the Landlord and Tenants Act puts a brake on any quite unjustifiable increase, but it does not necessarily go beyond this. Important factors, therefore, of this kind, which are quite beyond the retailer's control, must militate against more economical operations.

Alongside of this there has arisen a whole set of new standards of shop-fitting and shop-equipment. Some of these are very directly conducive to greater efficiency, as for instance the installation of X-ray machines in a boot department or of " daylight " lamps in other sections. In addition, there has undoubtedly been a social quickening of interest in architecture which is all to the good, and the reflection of this urge is bound to be present in commercial buildings. Its direction and control, however, is of very real importance, and while admittedly our achievements still lag behind the extravagant examples of certain Continental countries and of America, even our costs must represent at any rate an appreciable advance on the average unawakened experience of pre-war times. This is in part inevitable in an experimental stage, but that stage is not likely to be rounded off until far more logical thought is applied to the whole question. The functions

of shop-keeping and store-keeping certainly require adequate architectural expression, but the radical mistake
is that there has been no really concerted and co-ordinated
attack on the problem either by a competent body of
architects or of retailers. This has led to a considerable
amount of mis-spending on equipment and possibly to
a small amount of over-spending, but at the same time it
has curbed, through hesitancy and lack of assured knowledge, a probably still greater amount of proper and
desirable spending.

As in other matters, public demand plays its part.
Amenities, niceties and new attractions have come to be
expected ; and in many cases a refusal to swim with the
stream can quickly mean a definite loss of business. It
is, moreover, fair to claim that twenty years ago shops
were in many directions shabbily fitted out and a more
adequate outlay under this heading was therefore overdue.
The same point arises with the question of lighting,
which requires consideration as an expense from two
angles, first of its installation cost, and then of its consumption cost. Scientific discoveries have brought to
hand new possibilities—for instance in display lighting
—that cannot be ignored ; nor will a nice calculation in
1932 of the proper appropriation for lighting costs stand
for long, so rapid is the change in the comparative standards. Even to-day, for instance, Berlin's model kilo-
watt load per 100 feet run of show-windows is strikingly
ahead of London both in conception and cost.

In another direction—although this is partly due to a
beneficial change in accountancy practice—to-day's allowance for depreciation needs to be higher than heretofore.
It has been borne home on this generation that large cities

in particular will need re-planning and re-building more frequently than has previously been the case. The pace of development is such that it may soon be wise not to put more than a forty years' expectation of life on a building ; otherwise it may prove a clog upon the progress of the future. Just, therefore, as manufacturing practice has for some time past made provision for a rapid writing-off of machinery, a similar and partially new charge for obsolescence has now entered into the retailer's outlook, whose premises and equipment have equally to march with the progress of the age.

This realisation, coupled with a growing appreciation of the need for the provision of capital redemption funds in advance of the requisite time, will certainly be of very real service to the future, but its immediate upshot is a considerably enlarged debit against the present.

To sum up, therefore, the occupancy charge mirrors far more closely than might be expected the social tendencies of its environment. The quality of the building's initial erection, the pace of its continuous renovation, the date of its eventual demolition, are conditioned to a large extent by that changing environment, and the heaviest portion of its charge is directly or indirectly fixed in advance. The particular circumstances, or perhaps the methods of accountancy employed, may tend to obscure the true position, but it is likely that in sum total the outlay on occupancy (in accordance with the very comprehensive definition given above for rent, rates, interest on equipment, and all stages of maintenance and depreciation) may entail a 5 per cent. charge on the selling price of the retail product. It can, and does, rise well beyond this figure where " pitch," as for example with many multiple firms, is of outstanding importance. But in such cases the excess incurred may be to a considerable extent counter-balanced by savings effected through the absence of any large expenditure on advertising.

Publicity Expense

This last point will again serve to illustrate the inter-relation between the different types of expenditure, and brings us at once to a consideration of the third " selling weapon "—Publicity. On the face of it, the expenses falling within this group are far more controllable in the sense that the budget is reviewed annually ; but the fruits of advertising are so dependent on a consistent and continuous line of policy, that in effect the appropriation set aside almost inevitably tends to hover round a definite percentage, and control of the expenditure is then con-centrated on the best allocation of the sum voted.

The apportionment between the three main channels : (1) Press and hoardings ; (2) Catalogues and direct mail ; (3) Display windows and internal " features," will, of course, vary according to individual requirements. The last-named, for instance, will assume greater importance in popular thoroughfares. Indeed, there are one or two striking instances, even of departmental stores, which rely almost entirely upon their windows (as is, of course, quite a general custom with the multiple shops), and exclude other forms of advertising.

In dealing with Press publicity a further nice balance has to be struck between the specific advertising of selected merchandise and that newer growth, publicity devoted to a general envisioning of a store's many-sided activities. This carries with it a study of the suitability of the media available and an analysis of their pulling power in relation to the cost of their space.

The average individual expenditure by stores has probably been fairly steady for some time past at about 3 per cent. of sales turnover, although quite ordinary variations from 2 to 4 per cent. will be found; and possibly half of this outlay has been commonly devoted to Press advertising.* Undoubtedly, however, the actual revenues that now accrue to the newspapers bulk far heavier than in pre-war days. There are many more advertisers; larger trading units generally are operating; and the higher level of prices has up to now been supporting a greater outlay without any noticeable change in the percentage allocated. These causes have probably blunted scrutiny of the disquieting fact that in the last decade rates of space in the national organs have been steadily rising against the retailer without anything like a corresponding increase in traceable results. Indeed, the reverse process is in evidence in some quarters. It is, of course, not unexpected that artificially inflated circulations of this type are very far from producing *pro rata* returns; and the newspaper proprietors may well have to recognise this growing burden and to modify their present conception of making the advertising revenue foot the news' bill to such an undue degree.

Meantime the distributor also will need to adjust his mind. As an individual he will have to frame his yearly

---

* This figure does not include the rental space of show-windows, which is, however, sometimes charged up against the individual departments in one's internal accounts.

budget in the light of these changing conditions. Already, probably, there has been a certain swing over to the other forms of publicity; and there is no doubt that the technique of window display is making very great strides. But the trade as a whole—as distinct from any individual member of it—is likely to be judged on its realisation of a more radical issue. The scale of the national Press organs is, in fact, a challenge to the distributor to widen very greatly the circumference of his own scale. It is, for instance, an obviously worth-while proposition to-day to advertise in the national papers certain articles of universal consumption, and in some cases a manufactured brand will answer this description. The same, of course, applies to the advertising of a firm whose name is a household word. The gap, however, between these examples and the ordinary case of the retail publicist, with his strictly limited appeal, is far too great to be complacently accepted. In one way or another, stage by stage, this gap will have to be bridged and avoidable waste eliminated. For this purpose co-ordinated action is a prerequisite, exactly as was found to be the case with the problem of site values, of buildings and equipment. To this problem we can return in later chapters.

Expenses Summary

Although these three groups cover the most important items of expenditure, they do not, of course, pretend to form a complete list. Outside them, for example, comes the by no means negligible charge for the various forms of despatch—by van delivery, and by carrier, rail or post. There is also the purchase of stationery, of packing and

of other consumable supplies ; and a considerable aggregate total for administrative matters such as telephones,
insurances, welfare, debt collection and bad debts, together with professional fees for legal and audit services.
It is particularly difficult to be very definite about the
sum total of these miscellaneous charges, but very possibly
the typical average range would vary from 3 to 5 per cent.
Although individually small by comparison, each item will
none the less be subject to severe and periodic scrutiny.

Nor does the control of any of these groups cease with
the more or less direct methods of analysis already described. There is simultaneously a constant exercise of
cross-lines of attack upon the figure problems involved.
For instance, one of the more important records to be
kept affords daily and weekly track of the output per sales
assistant, and another may illustrate the expense ratio of
selling to non-selling staffs. It might again be found ex-
pedient to charge up the departments with the supplies for
which they indent so as to secure economical usage ; or with
the floor space they occupy so as to ascertain the turnover
" yield " per square foot ; or with their advertising space
in order to keep a proper balance between them all. Or,
again, the trends of customer demand may be watched by
tabulating the average amount per transaction ; the percentage of cash to charge business, or the number and
percentage of returned parcels. In numerous ways,
therefore, a measuring rod is applied to test and promote
the efficiency of a business.

To attempt a complete picture of the figure result may
well be misleading, more particularly as we have taken as
our hypothetical example a store with a very comprehensive

run of services and a somewhat high ratio of expense. For such a store doing a really good-class business, well-organised, well-staffed, and well-equipped, offering the facilities of delivery and accounts and related services, we are probably left with middle figures for expenses somewhat as follows :—

Salaries and wages .	.	.	.	12½ per cent.
Occupancy	.	.	.	.	4½	,,
Publicity	.	.	.	.	3	,,
Miscellaneous .	.	.	.	4	,,
Total .	.	.	.	.	24	,,

A different standard of trading with a predominating cash policy may well show a saving on these figures to below 20 per cent., and it may further be useful at this juncture to repeat that the expense total given is in any case a more than usually inclusive one, as it not only makes provision in the occupancy figure for depreciation, but it also assumes—

1. An entry for rent on an adequate valuation, or alternatively in the case of an owned building an equivalent amount of interest, plus
2. In either case a similar " interest " charge on the capital employed in equipment.

This practice could not, of course, be followed for balance-sheets where any return on invested capital—apart from debenture interest—forms an appropriation of profits, and is not dealt with as a prior charge ; but it does give a clearer and completer picture from the trading point of view. It is, in fact, the most truly accurate picture.

Net Surplus

With an expense roll of this kind, it is probable that the realised gross margin will be in the neighbourhood of 28 per cent. We are thus left with a net margin of 4 per cent. on turnover, from which, in the first place, it will be appropriate to deduct probably not less than 1 per cent. as representing a fair rate of interest on the working capital employed in stocks and in liquid assets. By these means we shall have compensated the full total of capital subscribed to the business, but only on the basis of interest rates—neither more nor less—and we shall be left with not more than 3 per cent. as the resultant net surplus. It should be immediately noted that this percentage and other similar ones given in this chapter are always related to turnover, which, being the control figure for all operations, furnishes the proper clue to the *working* health of the business. It should not be confused with the dividend percentage, which is merely related to shareholders' capital,—an unreal guide in any case in that it may equally represent a considerable exaggeration or, conversely, an under-statement of the capital actually and actively employed in the undertaking. The Banks, for instance, pay a large ordinary dividend, because their issued capital in relation to the reserves which they have built up, and, in a different way, in relation to the magnitude of their daily operations, is small.

Generally speaking, it is believed that this " net surplus " of 3 per cent. should apply in normal circumstances to a progressive business, the conduct of which is distinctly above the average. The definition, it will be observed, is thus advisedly confined to an upper minority, except where results are appreciably assisted by the abnormal " windfall " of a low rental. It is further important to note that a parallel showing will occur in a cheaper and less intricate category of trade where an inclusive expense total of, say, 18 to 20 per cent. will move in step with a gross margin of, say, 22 to 24 per cent. In fact, on the basis of the definition above, it is thought that whatever the class of store trade this ratio of net surplus to total expenses and to gross margin should probably be fairly constant as a standard performance.

Moreover, this net surplus—over and above the bare return on their money that we have already allowed the shareholders—is worth consideration from several angles. As the trader sees it, first and foremost it is his safety margin. With operating expenses of 24 per cent., plus the further 1 per cent. assumed for " interest " mentioned above, he knows that a small series of miscalculations, or a slight tilt of the beam against him, would quickly reduce his 3 per cent. surplus to negligible proportions. And it should be remembered that any miscalculations or mis-fortunes give rise to a double set of adverse factors. For they nearly always take the form of a budget shortage on turnover, and this will speedily result both in a stock surplus that will need cutting to the detriment of gross margin, and also in an increased *percentage* of expense directly created by the deficiency in turnover. Conse-quently, the two movements together make heavy inroads into his slender margin.*

* A simple concrete example may lend point to this statement. The figures in column A give the standard performance which might be achieved on a budget of £1,000,000 turnover if everything went

Secondly, if he is prudent he views this margin as the chief source from which he can build up his reserves, subject always of course to the toll of taxes which will in any case seriously deplete the available sum.

Thirdly, it may well be a matter of quite legitimate pride to him if this sum, which, viewed in relation to his total expenses, contains only a relatively slight factor of safety, yet converts into a reasonably handsome percentage on the subscribed capital of the company because of the good use to which the latter has been put. For capital, too, is an instrument to be employed with vigour and with economy.

according to plan.   In column B the actual results are assumed showing :—

(a) A deficit in actual turnover of 5 per cent.

(b) A resultant small drop in gross margin, owing to stock difficulties, from 28 to 27 per cent.

(c) A curtailment in expenses set vigorously in motion half-way through the season when it was seen that the estimated turnover would not entirely mature.   Naturally, this could not quite keep pace with the turnover deficit of 5 per cent., but a saving up to $2\frac{1}{2}$ per cent. of the budgeted expenditure might be effected.

The net surplus, it will be observed, falls away from 3 per cent. in column A to 1·33 per cent. in column B.

	Standard Rate.	A. Estimate.	B. Actual.
Turnover . .		£1,000,000	£950,000
Gross margin . .	@ 28%	280,000	256,500 = 27%
Total expenses, including " Interest " .	,, 25%	250,000	243,750 = 25·67%
Net surplus . .	,, 3%	30,000	12,750 = 1·33%

To-Day and To-Morrow

CHAPTER XV

AN OBJECTIVE ANALYSIS OF RETAILING

UP to this point any detailed examination has been severely limited to one field of retailing—the departmental store. It has, moreover, been subjective in its method of approach, and it has isolated the individual merchant of a progressive type with a view to affording a preparatory understanding of the specific daily job with which this and that retailer is confronted.

Other than incidentally, it has not concerned itself with retailers as a body nor with retailing as a matter of national moment. Obviously, however, the retailer's position *vis-à-vis* the consumer calls for such an objective analysis, more particularly at a time when in many countries very widespread concern is being expressed about his performance of the function allotted him. In certain important respects the criticism is radically mis-directed. Accordingly value will attach to a preliminary clearance of some of the more serious misconceptions.

Perhaps the commonest form of such criticism is to the effect that, judged on the basis of pre-war standards, the level of retail prices has for some time past been out of keeping with the comparative level of wholesale prices. Further, that through the time-lag in the fall of retail prices this divergence has recently become more and more pronounced. Now the normal interpretation of the term "wholesale price" would be the price which is paid by the retailer to the merchant or to the wholesaler who immediately precedes him in the chain of distributive processes. From which it follows that the normal deduction drawn from any unfavourable divergence between wholesale and retail price levels would carry with it an implicit condemnation of the retailer as a self-interested obstructionist who is the sole cause of the sustained cost of living.

In real fact, however, the term "wholesale price" as technically used for index purposes very rarely has in view the price of the finished product which is bought by the retailer for sale to the public. Quite frequently, indeed, it has reference to raw materials, or at least to goods at one of the very early stages of manufacture. The more accurate approach, therefore, as will be seen from a glance at the Board of Trade's list of 150 selected articles, is to talk of "Commodity prices."

It will then be immediately apparent that at every intermediate stage of manufacture up to and including the actual retail sale itself, labour and other costs constitute a progressive load of relatively stationary charges, every one of which tends to "damp down" in the aggregate total any percentage variation that has arisen in the price of the original raw material. This "damping down" process, it should be noted, applies whether the price movement is upwards or downwards.

Professor Bowley, for instance, shows that the price of flour naturally moves less than that of wheat, and of bread less than that of flour, while a still more illuminating example is to consider the processes in the manufacture of clothing, each one of them contributing to a suspensory scaling down of any violent changes in the price of the raw cotton. The first stage of " ginning " is to separate the husk from the fibre. There then follow slubbing, carding and combing before it is ready for spinning into yarn ; after which comes weaving into cloth. The printers and finishers follow suit, and only then is it ready for manufacture into clothing. In a suit, a shirt or a frock, therefore, the actual value of the basic raw material is very possibly not more than 5 to 10 per cent. of the whole, so that even a landslide in the price of the primary product would not of necessity have a very great bearing on the price of the retail article.

Two actual examples should help to clarify the position :

MAN'S POPLIN SHIRT

Raw Material.	1930 Value.		Early 1931 Value.		Percentage Decline in Price.
	Price per lb.	Price per Article.	Price per lb.	Price per Article.	
Fine Egyptian cotton . .	@ 14·5d.	11d.	@ 10d.	7½d.	32
Fine mercerised yarn, 2/100s.	,, 60·5d.	3s. 4d.	,, 50d.	2s. 9d.	17½
Poplin cloth, 3¾ yds. . .	,, 20·6d. yd.	6s. 5d.	,, 18d. yd.	5s. 7½d.	12½
Finished garment * . .		8s. 5d.		7s. 7½d.	9½
Retail price .		12s. 9d.		11s. 6d.	10

* The finished garment in both instances includes a making-up charge at the rate of 24s. per dozen.

9

MAN'S SUIT

Raw Material.	1930 Value.		Early 1931 Value.		Percentage Decline in Price.
	Price per lb.	Price per Article.	Price per lb.	Price per Article.	
Raw wool, clean, 70s. quality .	@ 26d.	9s. 4d.	@ 17¼d.	6s. 2½d.	33½
Tops . .	,, 32¼d.	10s. 1d.	,, 24½d.	7s. 10d.	22¼
Yarn . .	,, 3s. 8d.	13s. 2d.	,, 3s.	10s. 10d.	17½
Cloth (buying in bulk) . .	,,14s. yd.	£2s. 7s.	,,12s.yd.	£2	15
Finished garment (factory made)		£6		£5 8s.	10
Retail price .		£9		£8	11

It will be noticed how insignificant an element is the cost of the raw material. In the case of the man's poplin shirt the proportion was only 7 per cent. in 1930 and has dropped to 5 per cent. in 1931 ; while in the case of the suit, the figures are even smaller— 5 per cent. and 4 per cent. respectively. Further, both examples show very clearly how the various stages of factory processing, largely by reason of the dominant wage factor, flatten out the downward curve of prices.

Obviously, therefore, it is necessary to move with circumspection before attempting any comparison between the Commodity Index and the Cost-of-Living Index, remembering that in the first place, the list of articles and their relative weighting is not the same for both indices, and, secondly, that the greater the amount of manufacturing transformation required to convert a raw material into a finished product, the more noticeable will be—

(a) the " damping down " of any retail price movement ;

(b) the prolongation of a time-lag prior to the start
of such a movement.

Other things being equal, the suspensory factor in any
price-adjustment is largely conditioned by the rate of
stock-turn within each intermediate stage of manufacture
and distribution. In times of falling prices, therefore,
the advantage under this heading is always with commodities, such as food articles, which pass into rapid
consumption. Contrariwise they will advance most
rapidly and strikingly when commodity prices are on
the increase.

Further, the shortcomings of the Cost-of-Living Index
itself should not be overlooked. As a measurement of pre-
war working-class budgets it may once have been reasonably adequate ; but the changed conditions of to-day have
made it a very unreal indicator as to the general level
of retail prices. Before, therefore, attempting any cor-
relation of the two indices, it is really necessary to break
up all retail products into groups that have a roughly
consistent " life-history " both in their kind and in their
pace of transformation from the raw stage. With this
done it should then be possible to prepare graphs that
would furnish really valuable information on this complex
problem. It is unfortunate that to date very little research of this kind has apparently been carried on,
although it may be mentioned that a limited enquiry
into food index numbers over the period 1924-29 has
been reported on by Professor Bowley,* and in that case

* Lloyds Bank Limited Monthly Review, June, 1930.

the " expected " or theoretical figures based on a mathe-
matical formula that had its birth in a pre-war experiment did very closely coincide with the actual movements
of prices, thus suggesting that a scientific study might
provide reliable data in striking contrast to the generalisations which are so indiscriminately broadcast by the
ill-informed.

A second line of criticism has as its basis for attack the
very noteworthy increase in the number of distributive
employees,—a factor which, taken by itself, might easily
lend colour to the suggestion that wastes in distribution
are on the increase. For, on the face of it, the position
is that between 1923 and 1930, during a time when the
total insured population in work remained practically
stationary—the rise being only from about 10,180,000
in the former year to 10,490,000 in the latter—distribution in the wholesale and retail trades has apparently
increased its insured pay-roll from about 1,180,000 to
1,620,000.

These figures, constituting as they do nearly a 40 per
cent. increase, obviously call for an examination of the
social and economic factors at work ; but in the absence
of any evidence that is capable of definite proof the best
that can be done is to submit as impartially as possible
certain tentative suggestions which in their sum total
may go a long way to explain the position :—

(a) The figures only deal with the insured workers, so
    that if, as is known to be the case during the
    years in question, there has been a considerable
    disappearance of the small employer who was
    outside insurance, and he has been replaced by

the insured employee of, for example, multiple firms, the total number of insured workers would be automatically swollen. Incidentally therefore these figures may in part form an interesting and favourable commentary on the recent permeation of distribution by large-scale organisation.

(*b*) One of the more important factors to which distribution should normally bear some relation is that of total population. It is estimated that this increased between 1923 and 1930 by about 6 per cent.

Moreover, in the same period there was great activity in the building trades, giving rise to about 1,500,000 new houses. This was accompanied by a considerable transfer of the population to new areas, and remarkable extensions on the circumference of large towns. A spread of shopping localities of necessity followed suit.

(*c*) The degree of service expected of the distributor also affects the amount of employment in his trade. To take two examples alone, delivery is nowadays more widespread ; and the counting-house is also a bigger factor, sometimes through the growth of the ordinary type of straight credit transaction, sometimes through the channel of instalment buying.

(*d*) The national income is more widely diversified, and the purchasing power of the working classes considerably increased. This is important, because an improved status for those either on or a little above the subsistence level can give a far greater impetus to the purchase of consumable goods than any increase in the higher ranges of income. This post-war trend has been accentuated by a very considerable shift in social habits. It would, for instance, probably be accepted that of recent years there has been progressively less and less of the old-fashioned form of saving, and that consumer-spending in the aggregate, having many more wants to satisfy, has been taking place on a more generous scale.

(e) This major movement has been accompanied by other contributory factors. For example, durability in an article is not the asset that it was. Goods at a lower price and with a shorter life are definitely in demand, so that purchases have to be made more frequently ; and in women's wear particularly not only has there been the call for the increasing variety of fashion, but home-dressmaking has given place in considerable degree to shop buying of ready-to-wear garments.

(f) Again, a whole run of new activities has been establishing itself. The motor car, the gramophone and wireless, starting as luxury articles, have now passed into fairly general consumption ; and service activities, such as that of hairdressing, have come right to the front.

This change in the trend of social habits of spending produces interesting if different parallels in other trades.

For example, during the period in question, insured employment on trams and buses has risen from about 105,000 to 155,000, in hotels and clubs from about 230,000 to 310,000, and in laundries, dyeing, etc., from 100,000 to 130,000. All of these activities, it should be noted, are closely dependent on the public's habits : and the significance of a comparable movement in each of them is inescapable.

The supposition is therefore that there has been greater recourse to travel by bus and tram ; to the use of hotel, boarding-house and club ; of laundries and dyeing ; and similarly that there has been a greater volume of retail trade through social changes affecting the proportions of total income allocated to spending of this type. The same phenomenon, in fact, appears throughout Western Europe and America, where the mass-production of many new types of goods has created a new set of conditions for the distributor.

In Germany, for instance, the census figures for persons employed in distribution (both retail and wholesale) showed a total of 3,115,608 for 1925, whereas in 1907 there were in the area at present occupied by Germany only 1,995,684. (In the area originally occupied the number was 2,100,430.)

With regard to the United States, Professor M. P. McNair, of Harvard University, reports that the preliminary census total for 1930 " indicates that 7,537,000 persons were engaged in distribution as against 4,243,000 in 1920. Over the ten years apparently the number of females employed in distribution increased from 668,000 to 1,716,000, while the number of males increased from

3,575,000 to 5,820,000. These figures are, of course, rather rough and perhaps not wholly reliable.

"One probable reason for the increase in the proportionate numbers engaged in distribution lies in the fact that in production industries the power of the worker has been tremendously multiplied by the power of the machine with consequent increase in per capita output, whereas in the marketing field no such development has taken place. We manufacture merchandise on a horsepower basis, and still distribute it on a man-power basis. Take, for instance, the petroleum industry, which had a rapid development in the United States between 1920 and 1930. The number of persons required to handle the wholesale and retail distribution of one thousand gallons of gasolene is manifestly greater than the number required to produce one thousand gallons of gasolene."

Accordingly there would appear to be reasonable ground for holding that the criticisms first of retail prices, pre-war and post-war, and secondly of the rise between 1923 and 1930 of those employed in distribution are, when taken strictly on their basis of comparative standards, largely mis-directed and have their uses mainly in the fact that some of the answers given to these criticisms may of themselves get us nearer to the real heart of the problem.

In the ultimate analysis we are faced with this line of attack, that the disparity between the price of the raw material and that of the finished article is prima facie evidence of excessive costs at some or all of the various stages of production, distribution and sale; and that, in any case, a disproportionate amount of the final price is taken up in retail charges. An examination of that criticism is called for.

Let us proceed to do so by considering, in the first place, how far the present framework of distribution corresponds to its social environment. A bird's-eye view of the country shows a population of about 45,000,000 ; sometimes gathered together in greater or lesser nodal points,—towns large or small ; sometimes stretched out in ribbon development or scattered widely over outlying districts. To a very large extent shopping areas are similarly disposed, most thickly aggregated in those magnets, the large cities, where there is roughly one shop to every ten or twelve houses ; but also found in plentiful supply even in small villages. Their number probably exceeds the very high total of about 500,000, thus giving on the average more than one shop to every hundred of the population, men, women and children, or about one shop to every twenty houses.

The root idea has obviously been convenience of location for the shopper, and this theory of convenience has similarly found expression in other directions as well. For once it is granted that every retail sale is the satisfying of an individual want, one advances by easy stages to admitting the possibility, if not of 45,000,000 kinds of wants, at any rate of a prodigious number of varieties,—the want being expressed differentially not only in the category and class of article, but also in the kind of service, occasion and circumstance attached to it.

It then follows that the regulation of one's business will be rendered subject to the conflicting cross-currents of highly irregular shopping hours, shopping habits and shopping tastes. Conveniences grow quickly into comforts, tastes into whims, fashions into fancies ; all of them leading to a dissipation of effort, and in the last resort defeating the primary object of convenience itself, which may be defined as usefulness at a reasonable cost.

The citation of these ever-present tendencies in distribution may seem trite because the danger confronts every age, and to a lesser or greater degree all types of civilisation. It provides, however, a useful jumping-off ground for the examination of our particular problem in that the recent advent of mass-production has accentuated the inherent difficulties of distribution. For the economy of machine-power should reside in its concentration at 100 per cent. continuous pressure ; and this can only be achieved where the buying weight of the distributor can set the pace. Where therefore conditions exist that are inimical to such concentration, and hinder the employment of the machine up to capacity, we are running counter to first principles. This then constitutes the acid test for the whole of twentieth-century industry.

But first it may be well to take one or two typical cross-sections of present distribution so as to get a clearer idea of the complexities involved. In the *Economic Journal* for September, 1929, there appeared an article on Retailing, by Mr. W. R. Dunlop, which included some interesting statistics for shops doing a good trade in certain smaller provincial towns.

The investigation was only possible within narrow limits, and the samples taken were comparatively few and to some extent haphazard. But the figures are well worth re-quoting even although they have to be accepted with reserve, e.g. the size of the furnishing turnover, or the estimated figures in column 8. Columns 1-8 are copied exactly from the article in question, but columns 9-11 are now added, being further deductions from the original figures.

The table on next page immediately illustrates the astonishing variety of retail conditions and the danger of too ready generalisations upon the trade as a whole. For instance, the sale of newspapers, with everything in its favour in the way of a standard article, negligible stock and a high roll of regular customers, nevertheless poses a difficult problem in its £. s. d. turnover because of the trifling value of each transaction. As a consequence, when we come to newsagents' expenses, there will be a high rent percentage despite a modest rent figure in itself, and an awkward employment factor in the relation of wages to takings. Moreover, the cardinal problem of low value per transaction is by its very nature permanent and outside control.

A very different set of circumstances faces the boot retailer, the acute trouble here being the slow stock-turn which is closely linked with the number of lines carried, and the small number of customers served in this trade which entails intermittent idling for the sales assistants. Here, whereas the second problem is only to a small extent controllable, the first for obvious reasons calls for vigorous handling, but is beset with difficulties ; more particularly as of recent years there has been a laudable movement towards better service by the supply

Trade.	1 Stock at Selling Price.	2 Rent.	3 Stock-turn.	4 Number of "Lines."	5 Salespeople.	6 Value of Purchase.		7 Number of Customers per Week.	8 Minutes to Serve.	9 Annual Turnover.	10 Salesperson Occupied per Week for	11 Turnover per Salesperson.
	£	£				s.	d.			£	hrs.	£
Grocery and Provisions	1,794	200	10	350	4	3	0	2,300	4	17,940	38	4,485
Meat	83	175	125	10	3	2	6	1,500	2	10,375	17	3,458
Tobacco	520	150	10	180	2	1	4	1,500	1	5,200	12½	2,600
Fruit and Vegetables	65	125	80	40	2	1	6	1,500	1	5,200	12½	2,600
Fish	29	125	200	15	2	1	6	1,500	2½	5,800	31	2,900
Confectionery	173	85	9	100	2	0	10	675	¼	1,557	1½	778
Newspapers	4	90	313	10	2	0	1	6,000	½	1,252	25	626
Millinery	260	200	30	50	3	15	0	200	10	7,800	11	2,600
Boots	2,995	240	2·5	150	3	12	0	240	6	7,487	8	2,496
Furnishing	14,976	500	2·5	125	5	120	0	120	30	37,440	12	7,488

of a far more accurate range of sizes and fittings. This, of necessity, entails a heavy stock, while the whole problem has been further aggravated by the rapid incursion of the fashion element into women's shoeing. To-day, therefore, a satisfactory modicum of stock is probably disproportionate to the size of turnover which can be anticipated in ordinary shoe shops. Further study of the problem may in fact point clearly to the adoption of a minimum turnover of £10,000 upwards as the economic unit for efficient shoe retailers.

Yet another point comes to light with the perusal of the confectionery figures where the amount of idle time, even should we as much as quadruple Mr. Dunlop's allowance in column 8, would still remain extreme. Frequently this is a trade only rendered possible when run in with the domestic life of the family. It is also said to be an instance where manufacturers definitely encourage the multiplication of selling outlets, acting presumably on the theory of the recurrent drop of water that the temptation of four, five, or six sweet shops on the child's homeward journey is more likely to succeed than a smaller number. Here, therefore, the inherently uneconomic size and character of the unit may be offset for the retailer if his home and his trading activities can both be operated under one roof ; and for the manufacturer by the aggregate enlargement of the area of his sales.

Viewing now the table as a whole it is pertinent to distinguish between the variables and the relatively constants. The first class, for instance, if we look at column 3, shows a range of stock-turn stretching from the daily

replenishment of newspapers and the twice weekly replenishment in the food group down to little more than a
twice yearly "turn" in much of clothing and furnishing.

Contrariwise, in column 6 these trades example an
inverse ratio for purchasing value per unit,—the figure
of a penny for newspapers rising through an approxi-
mate average of 2s. 6d. for food purchases and of
something less than £1 for clothing, to several times the
latter total for furnishing.

On the other hand, there appears to be a relatively
narrow range of variation in the size of the small shop
as shown in the rent paid. (Naturally newspapers and
confectionery, on the one hand, may be classed as practically half shops, and furniture at the other extreme as,
so to speak, a double shop.) There is also within these
physical limits a fairly constant figure revolving round
three for the number of sales-people employed ; and,
again with the same natural exceptions noted, a turnover for sales-people averaging from £2500 up to £4000
per year.

Now the stability of the size factor in the distributive
unit is of cardinal importance. The table quoted represents certainly the upper strata of small shops and yet
examples a range of yearly turnover for food and clothing
units from only £5000 to £10,000 per annum, carrying
an ordinary pay roll of about three persons. If, however,
we were to take the vast bulk, the middle or lower strata
of small shops, it has been estimated that their average
takings must be placed below £3000 per annum : probably a total of £2000 is far nearer the mark. This is
a notably small return per unit, and its significance is

underlined when we consider that many of the multiple chains and to some extent the individual departments of the ordinary departmental stores will also show a normal figure of only £5000. Nor is it that this " belt " represents the economic limits within which the retailer can work most satisfactorily. In point of fact, it pinches and cramps most possibilities,—stock, personnel, and service ; and yet it undoubtedly rules throughout most of distribution, obstinately conditioning even multiple organisations which in other directions have been pre-eminently successful in achieving scale.

The picture is worth pausing on for a moment,— a typical small unit with an area of a few hundred square feet ; equipped with shop front, fittings and other installations ; demanding a working capital to be employed in carefully chosen merchandise and possibly also in a multiplicity of trifling accounts ; lit, heated and rated ; carrying a small but constant staff ; and for all this only showing a grand total of about £10 trade per day.

It is essential therefore to consider what are the predisposing causes which so dominate the situation. A haphazard jumble of causes perhaps ; but at root there is most powerfully at work the public's innate desire for its " shop round the corner " ; and more than that, a choice of shops, on the theory that competition always pays ; and overlaid on this again the first fruits of mass-production which has made it easier to produce than to sell, thus reinforcing from the other end the illogical urge to open more and more shops.

It is waste of time to attempt to fasten blame for this state of affairs. There would be a considerable measure of truth in the statement that as retailing mirrors the state of society about it, to that extent, equally with politics, the public gets the form of distribution it deserves.   But that way lies complacency and inertia.   The urgent need is, first, to be wide-awake to the fact that an excess of shops means a very burdensome locking-up of idle capital and a locking-up of human energy, and, secondly, to consider how far this slack can be taken up.

Let us make no mistake about it ; this is the most difficult problem of all in distribution, precisely because a control of conveniences or limitation of choices, where it touches the daily individual life and purses of the whole population, so easily runs counter to certain very deep-rooted instincts in human nature. Further, of course, it must be admitted that up to a point a reasonably good case can still be made out for a wide spread of distributive outlets.

It may, however, be objected right away that, even granted this alleged excess of shops, the law of supply and demand will come in as a self-adjusting mechanism and sooner or later correct the position. But does it ? To start with, the average level of performance is depressed without being too obvious to the eye, because the excess consists not in shops that are shut but merely in shops that are not fully employed. It is different from house-property where the " To Let " notices immediately help to distinguish empty from occupied houses. Accordingly, in the sheltered industries, whether manufacturing or distributive,—just as in a profession,— overcrowding generally leads to a smaller share all round, but not to any rapid weeding out.

And further obstacles occur. In any case, of course, this theory of the equation of supply and demand is easier of application to commodities and liquid values than to fixed assets. The railways provide a classic example. One can write down the value of the goods on one's shelves and so dispose of them, but the shelves themselves are kept and the shop doors remain open in the hope of being fully needed again.

Meantime, in an age when the sale of goods becomes more difficult than their fabrication, there is a natural tendency to meet the difficulty of disposing of these outputs by increasing the pressure of salesmanship. This both sustains the present number of shops, in that competitive distributors can be offered competitive brands and articles, thus repeating in the retail field the overlapping and lack of standardisation that is rampant in the manufacturing field ; and, furthermore, it not infrequently adds to the number wherever multiple chains and manufacturers themselves open up new outlets.

Let us consider, for example, the birth of any new district. Before even the houses are half built, it is the business of the estate agents to ensure a " representative " run of new shops in the main centre, this representation being all the more worthy if it can offer the spice of a competitive showing between some of the leading multiple chains. Moreover, these shops will form only the nucleus, with the object that they in turn can act as a guarantee that in due course a ribbon growth of other shopkeepers adorns the less central pitches.

In this way it comes about that for upwards of ten miles in and out of London, north, south, east and west, every main thoroughfare is littered with a jumble of shopping areas ; budding, in being, passé, derelict. The process of decomposition covers perhaps a thirty years' span, but the end is tolerably assured.

Nor is this all. To increase the confusion, shopkeeping has a lure for those who are often both inexperienced and ill-equipped. It is believed to require little capital and to be comparatively safe ; and undoubtedly it often affords opportunity for a bare livelihood by giving over the front living-room, with services of wife and possibly child thrown in, to trading purposes. Viewed therefore in isolation from the general problem, this form of retailing can no more be condemned than other forms : it may at times even have its uses and its advocates,— as is also the case with yet other participants, the street hawkers and street markets. But inevitably in one way and another the process of subdivision and sub-subdivision goes on.

At this stage of the enquiry, before considering remedial measures, it will be useful to determine just how far the analysis has brought us. We have first taken it as axiomatic that the individual outlet in any one category of distribution is likely to be for the most part a small unit. On the other hand, we have suggested by implication that in all probability it is by force of circumstances frequently smaller than it should be, and that each trade and category of merchandise requires special enquiry so as to determine more closely, in relation to its location and other conditions, the economic size for its typical unit. We have been further faced by an overlapping in numbers that, by giving rise to wasteful competition and an amount of internal slack, probably more than any other single cause militates against economic working. Under this heading of overlap there would appear to have been no improvement whatever in the last decade, but rather the reverse. Retailers, manufacturers and public all have contributed to the waste. Each phase of society stands condemned ; and society is apparently making no serious effort to grapple with the complex problem.

The costliness of the failure in this direction brings a trail of penalties in other directions which has reacted to the retailer's discomfort, and has obscured much excellent progress that has actually been made. Indeed, despite the handicap of a general structure that is clogged and obsolete, within this framework there has nevertheless taken place in many ways a marked growth in scale, and a solid attempt at that essential simplification which is required to render effective the potentialities of mass-production. For while shopping convenience may reasonably entail a spread of selling outlets to satisfy single wants that in themselves are individually small, machine-power demands bulk purchase of the retailer. Where the logic of this idea has been seized on and a concentration of purchasing power has been achieved by multiplying a standard unit shop, there credit can justly be given.

Earlier mention of the part played by multiple chains in opening new shops might at first sight suggest that they had been invidiously selected for severe stricture, whereas it is in effect merely a comment on their un-usually vigorous development. Some seventy years back vision, determination and energy seized on the possibilities of this type of merchandising where goods were in daily and universal need and, with unerring skill, picked for the first experiment, provisions that could be easily packeted. From that first beginning has sprung one chain after another until pretty well the whole field of food distribution, perishable and non-perishable, is now in process of being covered. Side by side developed the first chemist chain of shops and the first newsagent chain. Then came the attack on clothing goods, which, if not in daily demand, were sufficiently repetitive to afford scope for standardisation,—shoes, hose, men's clothing and so on. Nor should it be overlooked that this standardisation, when properly used, actually can assist the chances of a well-assorted variety, for the reason that its orderly bulk enables the machine to work on an economic run.

The scale, therefore, of multiple distribution, of the departmental store, the " fixed-price " store, and the co-operative movement can all testify to a great advance in the technique of merchandising and general organisation. Each in their own way represents a twentieth-century adjustment to a very new set of conditions that have been created by urban development, by the march of transport facilities, by science and invention, and by a remarkable social re-orientation.

But while these recent developments may provide fingerposts for further advances in the future, to the thinking industrialist as to the outside critic neither production nor distribution has as yet solved the problem of organisation and of costs that the twentieth century is posing for them. To that extent the real burden of the criticism from which we started, that there are "excessive costs at some or all of the various stages of production, distribution and sale," lies unanswered.

It has been suggested that the community's own share of responsibility for the particular form of the riddle is no small one. It now remains to be seen whether there are not some indications for lines of solution, and whether the lever which is to the hand of distribution might not be a particularly powerful and salutary factor in the situation.

CHAPTER XVI

FUTURE TRENDS

THE root problem of modern economic life is posed by the separation of the producer from the consumer ; its root evil the obstructions we have set along the industrial roads that should carry products into daily use and enjoyment. In the internal layout and organisation of a unit factory we do not tolerate conditions that block the way or cause wasted effort and maladjustment, but we have yet to apply the same doctrine to the routing and processing of Industry as a whole. For that purpose the scale of planning and co-ordination will, of course, need to be far greater ; but once this has been achieved, the directer the flow, the more notable will be the final economy of effort.

In this scheme the retailer occupies a key position ; for as the representative of the consuming public he alone can transmute their daily purchasing needs into orders. It is for him, therefore, first to visualise and then to render effective for common use the potentialities of production. Of the four cardinal factors that condition his activities, we have concerned ourselves in the last chapter more particularly with two that act as heavy handicaps ; and we have seen that

(a) the whole management of his organisation is exceptionally liable to the disorder of individual tastes, hours, habits, etc.; and
(b) at every turn he is handling a multiplicity of single and trifling items.

We can now turn to the other two factors that benefit him :—

(c) Subject to the very important qualification that there is no vestige of control over the number of entrants into the field, he has a monopoly for serving the home market. Hence distribution is called a " sheltered trade."

(d) This market is relatively stable, its fluctuations from year to year being within a comparatively small compass, although over a period their aggregate effect may be considerable.

The opposing pull of these four factors can be seen definitely at work in the following broad figures :—

The advantages entail that about one-half of the total income of the country passes steadily and inescapably through retail hands, possibly up to a grand total of £1,750,000,000 a year. For measurement of its size this can be set for instance against the total productive output of the country, estimated in 1924 at £1,743,000,000, inclusive of utility services, or against 1930 statistics of £570,000,000 for exports and £1,040,000,000 for imports.

The disadvantages have in the past meant a dissipation of this turnover through upwards of 500,000 outlets, with an average number of about three employees per shop, and an average taking of £10 to £15 per day. Furthermore, it is probable that several hundred millions of capital are being employed, and the ratio of this figure to the total turnover mentioned evidences a wasteful locking up of money.

Accordingly, the constructive approach is obviously to turn our attention to the advantages mentioned, and to consider means for making the best use of them. It is too readily forgotten that the goods required by this 45,000,000 public in the home market are to a large extent daily and repetitive necessities, and these daily requirements, although individually presented, can be made to take much more of a common form. In fact, probably one-half of the spendings is in food and drink ; and a considerable portion of the residue is concerned with ordinary clothing and household needs. It follows, therefore, that any orientation of retailing that is directed largely towards the public, viewed as 45,000,000 separate and scattered individuals, is dissipating the potentialities that lie to hand. The orientation should rather be back towards a concentrated producer and a concentrated manufacturer, and the instrument for that concentration is undoubtedly the retail agent who can collect, classify and co-ordinate the staple wants of the consumer. But this work of co-ordination cannot be properly done so long as these wants have to filter through 500,000 channels, 80 to 90 per cent. of which are individually operated, and therefore individually ineffective for bulk purchasing.

This is by no means tantamount to saying that a mere enlargement of scale or bulking of purchases will get rid of all problems. Other incalculable hazards will remain ; for the appeal of price by itself is sometimes found to be surprisingly ineffective. Each retailing organisation again has its own particular niche ; and a conjunction of luck and soundness of instinct is required in the selection of the right means and occasion for creating a market. But despite all this, the essential fact of which the retailer should never lose sight, is that by virtue of his position he commands the approaches in both directions, and that he is thus enabled to actualise market possibilities and factory possibilities in terms of each other. The secret of the striking development since the war of all large-scale retailing, and particularly of the multiple organisations, lies in their grasp of this simple principle, and their adherence to it will ensure their inevitable future expansion.

Let us, for example, take the field of provisions and see how the " Virtuous Circle " can grow, once the grocer starts aright with his central idea. Over the greater part of his field he is selling goods that are packeted or tinned and not quickly perishable. Very well ; that is his first key to the position, for it provides him with the possibility of a range of standard articles. Then he has a further point of fixation by standardising his qualities ; and properly used this can be of double benefit to him, not merely in simplifying the variety of his stock, but also in winning repute for known and reliable articles.

Next he is reasonably assured of a very steady daily volume of business per customer, and this regularity can contribute to the economy of his wage, rent and delivery expenses. The aggregate of these helpful factors encourages still further recourse to standardisation ; and, providing, of course, that the number of selling outlets in a chain is kept within the limits of human control, their multiplication furnishes at each further step fresh possibilities of bulk merchandising.

Alongside of this, other avenues are being opened up. The pattern of the administrative technique has been worked out in the earlier stages, and therefore requires little more than repetitive extension as the organisation grows. The pattern of the shop unit, its layout and equipment, has been similarly evolved, and is similarly capable of reduplication, thus again combining economy of capital outlay with the hallmark of something that becomes known and recognisable.

And so the logic of development can proceed apace. Indeed, the elements of much of it can already be seen emerging in the grocery chains that exist to-day. The difficulty rather lies in the fact that these chains, even in this their most natural field of growth, do not perhaps number more than one in six of the full total of grocery shops, and the process of levelling up all the rest appears to be largely dependent on an exceedingly slow and haphazard pressure of events.

The example quoted also indicates what can be attempted *mutatis mutandis* in other fields. For wherever we are dealing with the necessities of life there will be found the opportunity for organisations that are capable of bulk purchasing, of which the most normal corollary is multiple selling. Natural produce (such as meat, milk, fruit, fish, vegetables) admittedly gives rise to certain acute problems of marketing, both because of its perishable qualities and because of its liability to alternating gluts and scarcity ; but these factors emphasise rather than belittle the need for organisation. If there are physical variations in the produce, the marketing solution lies in the first place with orderly grading ; if the complications of transport endanger safe transit or protract it, a planned regional campaign radiating from a centre is indicated. At every turn, in fact, large issues can only be settled by large-scale and co-ordinated marketing. This should be paralleled by similar co-ordination on the part of producers, with the object of securing the first step in a reasonable equation between production and distribution. The emphasis lies with the word " equation," and not infrequently conscious if imperfect headway in this direction is already being made.

It is seen, for instance, in the co-operative marketing attempts of the Grimsby and Hull trawlers, whose fishing fleets are now endeavouring to attain a reasonable measure of self-protection in a notoriously irregular market by entering into agreements direct with large distributive agencies. It is, however, still generally conspicuous by its absence from the marketing of home farm-produce, thus rendering largely nugatory any serious efforts to re-establish the prosperity of agriculture.

To illustrate the possibilities, let us for a moment assume that we have a clean sheet for the organisation of the milk industry, first taking in our stride certain favourable factors :—

(1) Milk is a standard commodity and (apart from specialised grades) saleable in a standard quality.
(2) It is the daily need of every household, and moreover in extremely steady demand from day to day.
(3) It is a generally recognised adjunct to health, and of particular benefit to children.

Starting with such initial advantages, one might expect to find some approach to a rational handling of the problem—experimental stations for concerted research in the breeding of cows, and in the production of milk quantitatively and qualitatively ; study of the right size of unit for the dairy farm ; the assembly of such units in relation to the pasteurising or distributive centre ; study of equipment and methods of sterilising, bottling and handling. At the next stage, one might postulate a run of distributive wholesale centres located with an eye to transport facilities and population needs, so as to ensure that each region received its milk with the least possible delay or unnecessary haulage costs. Radiating from these centres would be the retail depôts, each with a given run of streets to serve, regard again being paid to the elimination of wasteful overlap.

The whole could be backed by publicity that would carry the weight of medical and public opinion behind it, as soon as it was felt that on grounds of quality, hygiene, costs and efficiency the industry was operating to the best advantage. This pre-supposes a balanced integration of the industry that would have its starting-point in a recognition of their common interests and common responsibilities by producer and distributor alike.

It is, however, a picture far removed from the present state of disorganisation, where research work, if it is being done at all, is done for the most part in isolation ; where a minority of up-to-date farms rubs shoulders with the majority of backward ones ; where even efficient production is often left in mid-air for want of helpful marketing ; where there is little or no balance between the organised power of the farmer and of the retailer ; and where the purpose of such organisation as does exist is to protect the interests of one side against a supposedly inimical opposition.

Virtue attaches not so much to the particular form of the delineation as to its general intentions ; and the

underlying assumption is that with milk as with other
commodities historical accident has largely shaped the
haphazard form of its productive and distributive organisation. But is the imaginary picture very different from
one that might be reasonably drafted on a clean sheet ?
And if that is established, is it not well to have some such
set of governing considerations in mind when reviewing
the likely development of an enlightened milk industry ?
Nor should we overlook the immense leeway that has to
be made up, seeing that the British consumption of milk
per head is less than half the figure for the United States.

We require, therefore, a re-statement of the basic
factors before we can exploit to the full the natural
advantages attaching to a standard product of this kind.
The implications may at first sight seem novel in that
they appear to suggest acceptance of semi-monopolistic
corporations—at any rate, on the distributive side of the
milk industry. But it is immediately proper to observe
that a definite trend in this direction already exists to-day
with efficient organisations, such as the United Dairies
Limited, which have appreciated the inherent logic of
circumstances, and have acted with foresight, determination and ability in building on solid foundations. It is
true that they throw violently into relief a lack of pre-
paredness and skill in others, and that this entails a
state of disequilibrium which is fraught with grave possibilities of danger. It is true also that they themselves
have frequently been unable to surmount the obstacles
of a chaotic environment, and therefore forcibly repeat
on occasions the disorder that is present around them.
But where they have been fulfilling their essential function

of rationalising within its limited setting their own particular job, they are acting as signposts for the future. And if they do contain within them a degree of trustification which is capable of becoming burdensome by the abuse of its power, criticism for this lack of balance lies in the main against the backward and not the progressive units. Seeing, therefore, that milk is a national need, it is of vital importance to institute a complete overhaul of the general structure, and to work for a planned economy which will encourage a new technique of associated enterprise between the various parts of the industry. Its immediate objective and at the same time its justification in the eyes of the public, will be the very practical job of raising all-round efficiency and thereby reducing costs.

The same problem of potential costs faces us just as strongly in the field of manufactured goods, and here again it should be helpful to attempt to crystallise the conceptions which appear to be taking place in the minds of the more far-sighted industrialists.

Pre-eminently these leaders illustrate a capacity for thinking in terms of the needs of the machine. Let us explain this by reference to a ship's engine-room—trim, compact, purposive in its structure. All waste and excrescences have been consciously and ruthlessly eliminated ; the motive power stands out in its bare economy. Similarly with Industry, where the minds of the leaders —the engineer-architects—must be concerned with the erection of a simple framework, the sole purpose of which is to assist in expediting the processing of goods down all the stages from raw produce to finished product. The character, volume, pace, motivation of this processing is dependent to-day on the machine ; but in order to achieve volume, and thus to bring about an optimum level of costs, the machine in turn demands within the factory a standardisation of process movements and of specification and design. These requirements go hand in hand with continuity of output, which on the one side relies upon a reasonable stability in the raw material markets, and on the other side upon a flow of orders of a more or less uniform character. It is just here that the distributor can provide one of the keys to the situation. If he can mobilise and concentrate the community's needs in the desired form and volume without the impediments of unnecessary bottlenecks, he will set in motion a train of circumstances in which the machine can operate to the best advantage. In brief, the rationalisation of his own activities to suit the needs of the machine might well be the best and speediest guarantee for a parallel rationalisation in all stages of productive industry.

It has been laid down that a sufficient uniformity of consumer-demand is an essential. Do, therefore, the main categories of goods which we have in view suggest that this is possible ? To answer this we must first disabuse our minds of preconceptions that have their root in the confused merchandising practices of to-day, and secondly we must distinguish between a basic absence of uniformity and its mere superficial absence.

Put somewhat crudely,—while a structural absence of uniformity may be a primary and radical defect, decorative variations very probably are only a secondary matter. The same room, for instance, once its outline and proportions are fixed, is yet capable of many alternatives in the

way of decorative treatment.   Or, let us take a concrete
example from the shoe factory.   A whole run of goods
in different qualities, shapes and designs can be made
on welted plant.   The chief factor, therefore, in the economic running of a factory fitted up with such plant, and
having, say, a weekly capacity of 10,000 pairs, is the
ability to secure regular orders for 10,000 pairs of *welted*
goods.   Inside that output there are subsequent degrees
of variety,—differing heights of heel and shapes of toe
are of some consequence, as they call for differing lasts ;
of rather less consequence, in that it involves less capital
expenditure and fewer interruptions in process movements, are mere differences in patterns.   Still less, again,
would be changes in colours without changes in pattern.

Once this is properly appreciated, there is very considerable scope for variation in subsidiary factors without
affecting the vital principle of essential uniformity.   In
fact, the more we find it possible to materialise the
resources of concentrated standardisation, the wider the
field of orderly choice and differentiation can become
without any undue interference with economy.   Nor is
this all.   Only massed standardisation, owing to its
enormous output, can completely justify the employment
of the specialist in research, in design, and in marketing ; and over wide areas of demand it should therefore be
able to raise the general levels of taste and quality.   The
" cheap and nasty " stigma will, in fact, quickly be a
thing of the past once we have thought out the problem
of linking simplicity and excellence of design with standardisation in output ; and if examples are wanted as
forerunners, one may ask whether hose has suffered in

choice of material or texture or colour by reason of its mass-production, or cannot 1932 show printed cotton materials that in their design are a delight to the eye ?

It will be clear from the foregoing remarks that by reason of their purchasing power the fully developed multiple chains in particular possess natural advantages for making more fully effective the resources of machine-power. In the majority of cases they have confined themselves to a comparatively narrow range of merchandise, so that it is possible for them to operate almost as specialists with a well-defined size of unit for their outlet, and a well-defined category of goods for their supplies.

But the full measure of their purchasing advantage in the future will reside in a recognition of the vital interdependence between the activities of production and distribution. By these means the exaggerated horizontal alignment of industry which emphasises at each stage the potential conflict between buyer and seller will give way to a programme of continuous liaison. This principle of dovetailing has recently been described as follows : * " The distribution function includes responsibility for interpreting to the production function the specific needs and capacity of the effective and potential present and future market. It is responsible for co-operation with the production function in creating effective demand for the goods to be produced. It should provide the nervous system essential to the co-ordination of effort. This alone will secure that goods which are satisfactory to the consumer will be produced, sold and delivered at the

* Extract from a Report on Distribution by the International Chamber of Commerce.

time and place at which he desires them, and at prices
which will ensure the development of maximum demand
at least expense and with reasonable profit."

As an instance where the essential correspondence
between the needs of a shop and the potentialities of a
factory motivates a business, one might cite Montague
Burton, the multiple tailors, although in other ways the
case may not be very typical, as it illustrates a complete
vertical amalgamation of productive and distributive
enterprise,—a combination which is not frequently
successful.

In this instance, however, the factory is helped in
having control of a number of assured and successful
outlets ; in its strict limitation to one category of goods,
and, most significant of all, in its further concentration of
output on a fixed price (or quality) within that category.

It is indeed of interest that some of the most vigorous
examples of rapid chain development are to be found
among the " fixed-price " shops and " fixed-price " stores
whose adherence to the dominant idea of confining themselves to a small but definite range of price-levels has in
several instances enabled them to achieve remarkable
success.   In an earlier chapter mention has already been
made of the firm of Marks & Spencer.   In their case
the fixing of the arbitrary limit of 5s. as their maximum
price seems to have acted as a positive incentive to them
to bring a progressively larger range of merchandise below
that limit, and their operations now extend far into the
textile field.   All unnecessary intermediaries are eliminated and it is their avowed purpose so to integrate their
demands with the needs of the factories that on the basis

of massed orders running through at continuous pressure new low levels of cost can be established.

The raw material importer, the manufacturer of yarn, the maker-up, the technician, may all have to be called in for consultation with them so as to ensure the best possible utilisation of sources of supply, factory equipment, factory layout, and labour processes ; but the final results clearly demonstrate the savings that can be effected where intelligent marketing sets the pace for a correlated production.

In such cases there must, of course, be accompanying and restrictive adjuncts : there will be limitation of style, range and colour to those most in demand. There will be simplification of style, and there will be a ruthless refusal to dissipate effort over the occasional want. The same economy of idea will be seen in the surroundings of the store itself, and in the method of sale which frequently amounts to little more than a parcelling and handing over a counter. The bareness of this technique can in turn logically reflect itself in the type of sales-person to be employed. In other words, the goods are there largely to sell themselves : which they do by reason of their value.

Mass demand of this type is naturally focussed on the lower ranges of merchandise, but the root principles involved are capable of adaptation over a wide area through other types of organisation. Let us take, for example, the opportunities presented by the five or six leading provincial cities in the country. A social survey of those cities will indicate a large industrial element in their populations that range from 500,000 up to 1,000,000. In each case their size and status offers a promising field for the large departmental store, while their essential likeness of character may further suggest an experiment in a chain of related businesses.   And to take the process of reasoning a stage further—the chances of development for such a chain will largely depend upon strong central control and a concentration of buying resources.

That, in brief, would appear to have been the actual recent history of Lewis's Limited in Liverpool, Manchester, Birmingham, Glasgow and now in Leeds.   Exceptional courage was demanded, because it required a revolution in store technique to insist that buying could be concentrated in this way.   For how would a central office have the knowledge to buy successfully for Manchester and Birmingham and Glasgow alike ?   Or did the answer come pat to the effect that where Glasgow and Birmingham and Manchester led London by so much, there would be a blood-likeness in their superiority ? Whatever the line of argument, there has obviously been a deliberate scrapping of old ideas, and there is now clearly emerging an intellectual grasp of a new set of principles adapted to the needs of store merchandising for large industrial populations.

Mention so far has only been made of certain somewhat arbitrary examples of firms which, operating generally in the lower price-levels, have begun to realise the significance of machine-power in terms of cost and of economic satisfaction.   These, however, are only isolated examples which stand out against a general background that is confused and haphazard.   The problems of harnessing science and invention to the purposes of a *complete* industry still wait on the threshold, and in many directions those problems will be intensified where the productive processes are highly complex and the marketing of the commodity a skilled occupation. Indeed, the easy reaction is to assert that the principles outlined above are scarcely capable of application to such a case. Accordingly, it will be valuable to examine this proposition by selecting the boot and shoe industry.

For a proper understanding of the question we will choose for our jumping-off point the actual needs of the human foot :—

(1) The foot is a delicately contrived, cantilevered structure that has to support in maturity a daily burden of upwards of 100 lbs. of weight, and is therefore an essential factor in physical health.

(2) This structure has a covering of tissue and flesh with responses to motion and rest, heat and cold, support and restriction that differ according to each individual.

(3) It varies a great deal in its conformation, and for the first twenty years of life its rapid growth entails a series of changing problems.

(4) On twentieth-century roads it requires a protective envelope, sufficiently firm underneath to act as a shock absorber, and sufficiently supple on top to permit of reasonably free play. This envelope, therefore, must allow it to flex, stretch and breathe continuously.

(5) Leather, the material most suited for this purpose, is itself possessed of physical properties that react differently to different conditions. Moreover, it has to be subjected to transformations

in tanning, to mechanical stresses and strains in manufacture, and to yet another set of stresses and strains in wear.

Here is a complex of questions that very possibly are not capable of an entirely satisfactory solution. But they are questions that cannot properly be handled by the " hit and miss " methods of individualistic attack. They require a combined approach and scientific treatment. Until this is done we are obviously not providing anything like a clear run for the manufacturing side to get to work on the job that is proper to it. Indeed, one can imagine an arbiter who has been called in to recommend a rational constitution for the shoe industry submitting a statement somewhat as follows :—

" (A) My survey covers last-making, tanning, shoe-making and shoe-selling. It is a field that by its nature requires a series of interpretations from the processes involved in one stage into those involved in subsequent stages, and it is therefore of great importance that each section should work in the closest and freest co-operation with other sections. Accordingly, organised channels for such intercourse, which at present practically do not exist, should be immediately decided on.

" (B) Where there are so many unavoidable intricacies, it is of similar importance to devise a scheme whereby at the least a pool of essential knowledge should be made equally available to all accredited participants in the industry.

" These two main tenets give rise to three concrete recommendations :—

" (1) As the basis of good shoe-making is the last, I consider it essential to concentrate on securing a minimum but comprehensive run of first-rate lasts to take the place of the present multiplicity of overlapping and often indifferent models. To assist in this project there is an urgent need that a research body should act as the recognised clearing house for the classification of feet by measurement and type, and for the study of foot health and foot behaviour. It will require expert medical guidance. It should rely for much of its practical knowledge on data and experience to be furnished by the shoe retailer. Linked with this should be the complementary experience of the shoe manufacturer; and the whole should then be interpreted in terms of last models to be made in a strictly limited number of last factories which would serve the industry as a whole.

" (2) There should be similar correlated research on the properties and behaviour of the materials to be employed, and especially leather. This would have to cover every stage from the raw material to the finished product in wear. It would contribute to the rehabilitation of the tanning industry, and would greatly assist in solving many manufacturing difficulties.

" (3) In the manufacturing section much progress has been made with the relative standardisation of machinery, but this to be really effective, needs to be accompanied by a standardisation of layout and processing, under which the whole technique of the factory would be correctly adjusted to a particular class and volume of work. The aim would often be facilitated were groups of factories to get together for a pre-arranged apportionment of output according to type.

" By these means much will have been done to simplify the three basic needs,—last models, leathers, etc., and machine processing. Even so, production will remain infinitely diversified in its secondary aspects, but it will at least have its primary problems better regulated ; and it will consequently be freed for a concentration on its proper job of putting the goods through on the most economical run that is possible.

" Once this has been effected I can see the inherited skill of the different centres—Northampton, Norwich, Leicester, London, Stafford, etc., more advantageously utilised both for home production and for export. These localities would take concerted action in developing that type of product for which by tradition and experience each is more particularly suited : uneconomical factories would be immobilised ; and publicity, particularly for export, would be concentrated on the name of the centre itself. The marketing abroad of Northampton goods, for example, with the hallmark of Northampton upon them, could thus receive a notable stimulus.

" I have already suggested that one of the functions of distribution is to act as an intelligence service. In addition, its task in an organised industry of this kind should be to dovetail its activities with those of production by assisting in the elimination of unnecessary variables, by contributing to a regular flow of orders, and by allocating those orders systematically according to manufacturing type. An orderly marshalling of consumer-demand in this way should lead to an appreciable reduction in costs at every stage of the industry.

" My case for the above recommendations is that science and invention and machinery have presented us with opportunities that we cannot afford to fritter away, and have therefore made a re-assessment of our methods both necessary and inevitable."

Admittedly the particular form of re-assessment submitted would cut across some of the present main lines of historical accident, and would, therefore, arouse opposition ; but it has this of value in it as against any piecemeal consideration of just one or two aspects of the question that it does illustrate both the interdependence of the industry and the general direction of the problems posed by that interdependence.

Two typical objections that may be advanced against much of the preceding argument merit an answer. In the first place, there is the natural fear that standardisation leads to a dull level of uniformity in the product. Once, however, industry has mastered the technique of mechanism, this should prove to be largely a misconception. Indeed, it might be as apposite to argue that there can be no diversity of the human form simply because Nature has been wise enough for purposes of economy in effort to stereotype the essential organs and structure of the body. Where, therefore, in the case of articles of

apparel or equipment diversity is required in the secondary aspects of design, colour and adornment, this can be
best attained *for common use* by previously regulating the
wastefulness of any divergencies in the basic factors.

Secondly, it is contended that a bias in favour of large-
scale organisation implies an over-great belief in human
capacity ; and criticism is not infrequently directed to
the huge and amorphous concerns of the post-war period
which have failed to justify themselves. It would be as
well, therefore, to reaffirm two or three conditions without which large-scale industry cannot properly succeed.
First, the businesses that come together should either be
similar or else complementary in their general purpose
and character. Next, the individual unit of operation
should remain easily manageable in size. Finally, it will
be most important to define the field for centralisation
which, while leaving unimpaired their strictly local
autonomy to the constituent units, will at the same time
provide for co-ordinated control over any such matters
as supplies, research, administration and possibly marketing in which the needs of all the units may run parallel.

To take over a metaphor from architecture, " scale "
in a building denotes proportion and composition as well
as mere magnitude. Size in this sense is organic, and both
because of this, and because in industry it can facilitate
standardisation, it should be a very real factor in simplifying many problems.

Distribution calls for far more experiment along these
lines. Let the avowed object be to select and to simplify
for purposes of standardisation in essentials. For this
alone can lead to real economy, and if we secure in this

way a basic economy, then diversity in individual features will be justified, and can in any case look after itself.

As we have seen, the types of distribution which are more naturally fitted to this kind of development are those which limit severely the fields of merchandise in which they are operating, and also limit their range of prices and qualities. Having done this, the advantages can be pushed home by multiplying the outlets in a series of comparable districts. This is achieved either on the basis of

(a) Unitary merchandise, e.g. grocery chains, chemist chains, hose chains ;

or on the basis of

(b) " Bazaar " merchandise in one-price shops.

It would further appear likely that this trend will have a decided bearing on the future course of the departmental stores whose drawing power has hitherto been largely dependent on the extensiveness of their appeal, which in turn has helped to give them something of the character of social institutions. Naturally, the largest stores which are household names stand in a category by themselves ; but for all others their very extensiveness is in the future likely to hamper their competitive purchasing power *vis-à-vis* the intensive multiple retailer, unless they form themselves into small chains with central control of all staple merchandise. In that event their position should remain very strong ; and the provincial stores of Lewis's Limited have already been quoted as outstanding forerunners of this movement. In medium and high-price levels an alternative method of approach that offers itself in some cases will be to exploit the prestige attaching to their position by maintaining the individuality of their merchandise and of their general appeal. But even here they will have to reckon with the new possibilities of the multiple specialist. Hitherto the departmental stores have lacked nothing in alertness and vigour, so that there is no reason to suspect that they will be slow to keep fully abreast of changing conditions. The need for them to do so is great ; as they, more than any other single factor, can create a new shopping centre, or maintain the position of one that is experiencing difficult times.

This still leaves us with the numerically strongest class, —the small independent shop. Nor can we dismiss this merely as the shop that in the past served the parish well, so long as the horizon for most people was bounded by the parish. In many cases even in staple commodities it succeeds to-day on its merits by reason of its personal salesmanship, and this will to an extent remain true for the future, particularly in small towns and villages. But if there is anything in the contentions of the past few pages, the small shop's lack of purchasing power is for the most part already an anachronism, and one that will be in the near future gravely accentuated. It has already been seen how in America independent dealers, particularly grocers, have become so conscious of this handicap that they have been meeting the competition of the chains by the formation of voluntary associations, which obviously offer one form of solution for any continued widespread existence of the independent shop. Certain branded merchandise, on the other hand, can afford a different form of opening. Here the ground has been prepared by the active sales policy of the manufacturer, as in tobacco and cigarettes, and the retailer, who can in such a case quite conveniently be a small man, acts as little more than the distributive agent.

Taken by and large, however, the field for the small independent dealer will be confined more and more to merchandise where the element of fashion or individuality is of distinct moment. In other words, far more than in the past the type of product is likely to dictate the appropriate kind of distributive channel along which it should pass, and wherever its orderly assembly, flow and disposal can best be secured by large-scale organisation, this course will be increasingly followed as the natural choice.

To sum up, therefore, on the merchandising side, the cardinal thesis is that the marketing structure should have both its form and scale adapted to suit the varying needs of the different commodities that it has to handle ; that for this purpose its processes under modern conditions should be closely and continuously integrated with the processes of productive industry ; and that particularly for staple needs there should be a concentration on the standardisation of essentials so as the better to afford scope for diversity in any secondary attributes. In all sections of productive industry standardisation of this kind will be the surest precursor to a notable lowering of prices, and as a result on the distributive side the bugbear of slow-moving stock and the heavy costs of mark-down will be brought under far better control.

Parallel with this, certain developments will also become possible on the expense side. In earlier chapters we have seen that during the last generation social environment has tended to an elaboration and refinement in the trappings of distribution and that the costs of these trappings have been offsetting the economies effected by a better organisation of its primary purposes. To the initial expense item—the wage factor of personal salesmanship—there have been added growing charges connected with administration, with the building and its equipment, with publicity, with delivery and so on. It is, of course, clear that where there has been extravagant attention to these matters pruning is now required, and there must be a reversion to the more severely practical. But a wholly negative attitude would be a retrograde step ; the task rather is to utilise these resources with knowledge and discretion, particularly as the whole complexion of the problem is being altered by our general thesis. For an expenditure of effort and capital that was possibly burdensome in relation to a business of very moderate dimensions, becomes reasonable or capable of different handling when viewed in the light of a far larger organisation and a far larger turnover.

It has already been mentioned, for instance, that the multiple shop can work out a very effective model layout and can standardise on model equipment and fittings that are increasingly capable of economic handling because of their repetition throughout the chain. By comparison, the individual proprietor is committed to expensive methods of trial and error.

Advertising, again, is an instrument which calls for intelligent use. Helped by the fact that as a new form of activity it is not held fast in the grip of a strait-jacketing structure, it has in many ways definitely outdistanced distribution in scale. The upshot is that national advertising is for the most part only justified by products of national scope ; otherwise its costs become burdensome because they cannot be sufficiently spread. It demands, therefore, from its users that their outlets should bulk sufficiently to drive home the campaign up and down the country. Only a national brand, a prominent multiple organisation, a departmental store that is a household word, or a group of smaller stores linked in some form of associated publicity, can satisfactorily fulfil this requirement.

The same reckoning applies in many other directions. Whether it be a matter of office systems and office machinery, or the installation of new window-lighting, or the choice of delivery vans, it is necessary to make careful study and on occasion to enlist expert and costly advice out of all reasonable proportion to the likely results. Moreover, once the purchase has been made, the experience gained is often unlikely to be called upon again, unless the organisation is an outstandingly large one.

It is apparent therefore that we have outgrown our average channels of distribution as we have outgrown our average channels of production. Overheads have become top-heavy and require challenge, not so much by comparison with past results, or on the basis of present environment, but in the light of potentialities that are waiting to be utilised. Consequently for each group of commodities in turn it should be well worth while to attempt to map out a standard performance —not merely that bare level of performance as will support the present methods of handling merchandise, but an optimum that pre-supposes an organisation scaled to the pitch of productive industry.

In this way " bogey " figures could be set up to illustrate the turnover (or productivity) that could, for example, be achieved per £ of capital, per foot of space occupied, and per head of staff employed. Such a schedule of figures would undoubtedly throw much fresh light upon the whole difficult problem of expenses.

The standard performance must, however, have regard to a shop that is fully engaged, at any rate as far as is consistent with reasonable shopping habits; and this brings us back to the over-riding problem of the number of retail outlets.

The problem is peculiarly intricate, because it contains within it a conflict between opposing sets of realities. On the one side, there is an array of mainly psychological factors : on the other side there are economic dictates. Both equally have their basis in a reality with a one-sided truth to it, and the task is, therefore, to evolve some reasonable adjustment between the two.

Some of the psychological factors which contribute to an excess of shops by discouraging any curtailment even of superfluous opportunity and convenience may be worth recapitulation from an earlier chapter. At times they caricature themselves in queer little oddities—excrescences on the face of retailing—which by their very exaggeration lend significance to the fundamentals of the situation. There is, for instance, the customer who regularly shares her orders between two grocers, so as to keep both up to scratch, and then occasionally bestows her favours on a third to teach them both a lesson. There is the shopper who will take her long-standing custom elsewhere, because shoes that show unmistakable signs of having been burnt are claimed by her to have been made of disgracefully poor leather : or because, when shopping at the last moment, she meets with an inability to send along the goods by special delivery. Another always suspects the first piece of meat placed before her, and proceeds petulantly to see the full selection before returning to that originally submitted. Mrs. " Deeply Incensed " closes her account and will go elsewhere (events sometimes miscarry !) because she is politely reminded that her account is three months overdue. Perhaps most difficult of all are Mrs. Jones and Mrs. Smith, who always like to shop together ; and when they have both debated, and coaxed, and quarrelled for half an afternoon over a frock for Mrs. Jones, Mrs. Smith places an embargo on the shop and insists that they try again further down the street.

Such eccentricities as these are the extreme product of a very personal contact between salesman and shopper that can give rise to a species of petty tyranny with far-reaching results ; but except that it is applied with greater discrimination, even the more normal psychological attitude similarly implies an untrammelled freedom of choice on the part of the consumer as to place, time and circumstance ; and this is the pivot on which so much turns. For the desired freedom of choice can be only too readily made available at a period when the urge to find new or increased outlets for their goods is pressing on manufacturer and retailer alike.

There are other concomitant factors to reckon with. The tempo of change and of varying fashions has markedly quickened in this generation. There has been a redistribution of effective demand as between essential goods and whole new ranges of "optional" products, thus intensifying the alternative claims upon the consumer's purse. Improved transport has brought with it the possibilities of far more fluid purchasing, in place of relatively fixed habits in shopping. New housing estates again have meant a greater spread and to some extent a duplication of distributive outlets. All of these causes lend encouragement to a profusion of shopping facilities, and the psychological background has given rise to a change in emphasis from the old outlook which said " This need is not being met," to one which to-day says " This latent desire should be stimulated and catered for." Naturally also the difference shows itself not merely in the types of merchandise sold, but in the trappings and attractions with which the sale has to be invested.

To ignore or to minimise this reality of a changed psychology would obviously be to court disaster ; but what is apparently being overlooked is that changed economic factors present an opposing set of equally stern realities. We are faced with a nearly stationary population, and are thereby deprived of that automatic access of consuming power which can give a fillip to the expansion of industry. We are faced with a national income that at the moment is not even stationary, but according to the generally accepted estimate has probably shrunk since 1929 from about £4,000,000,000 to £3,500,000,000. And yet with the signal set at danger, and at a time when the surest hope is in concentration, we are standing by while a combination of circumstances is certainly maintaining, if not adding to, the multiplicity of distributive outlets. We appear, therefore, to be blinding ourselves to the fact that there comes a point where an increase of competition in a relatively sheltered industry is failing in its presumed purpose ; and is as likely as not to assist in raising prices by adding to the expenses of winning business. In such circumstances, forced liquidations do not apply over a sufficiently wide area to restore the balance. Indeed, so easy is it to enter into retailing, that there is always a short-lived newcomer—probably subsidised—to take the place of the outgoing failure.*

Surely the simple arithmetic of the position is that unless and until we find an improved economy for production and distribution, so as to make a given amount of money do more, there is only so much to go round ; and that an excess of shops means shops that are underemployed, which in turn means personnel and capital that are wastefully locked up. This may well lead us to the opinion that with retailing as with productive industry the first step in taking up the slack is deliberately to assist in the immobilisation of the inefficient unit, with a view to a better mobilisation of the efficient.

* *Note.*—There is the possibly apocryphal story of a representative of a prominent wholesale house who at the year's end appeared before the management to receive severe criticism on his handling of his particular retail territory. He was adjudged to have been deficient in energetic salesmanship because the bad debts on the accounts for which he was responsible reached such a very low total. By that token it was held that he could not have pushed turnover hard enough.

Nor should we ignore the very substantial advantages which could tell in our favour. We possess a key factor in that Great Britain has a relatively concentrated population of about 45,000,000, more than 60 per cent. of whom live in towns of over 25,000 inhabitants, and have a standard of life at least ahead of any country in Europe, —that standard, in fact, expressing itself in a consumer demand of about £1,750,000,000 per annum. We have also behind us a technique and tradition of manufacturing skill that has until quite recently been unrivalled. It needs encouragement to-day ; it needs to be made more flexible and more alert ; but unless distribution contributes its full weight to this end, we are shirking the economic realities, and to the extent of our default the standard of living will become depressed. This will in turn react to the disadvantage of distribution.

Undoubtedly varying methods and degrees of adjustment will be needed to bring the psychological aspects of consumer-demand more into line with modern economic requirements. One has to take into account the differential factors of commodities, localities and social classes, but in every case a prime necessity will be to attempt a really scientific analysis of market possibilities. Indeed, apart from efforts made privately and on a limited scale, there has been to date no adequate statistical study in order to evaluate the purchasing power of any particular community, and to assess its character and quality. There are equally no specific data available to indicate the relative weight of spending even for each of the major commodity groups. We cannot, for instance, put a figure to the public's annual purchases in, say, women's outerwear or groceries or shoes. There are no regional surveys or city surveys to indicate, on the basis of total turnover or of aggregate floor-area, whether in this commodity or that any given district is well served or too choc-a-bloc with shops.

But until we have some such general background of definite knowledge, we are obviously working very much in the dark, and there is bound to be a certain absence of direction to our energies and enterprise. It is not merely that the prospective newcomer to a district or that the isolated entrepreneur has to fall back upon a " spot " judgment which may or may not be right : what is far more important, no periodic and authoritative data are forthcoming to indicate to all interested producers, distributors and advertising experts alike that in its wealth, its factors of population, its transport and trading facilities the relative showing of a district is by comparison with others above or below average ; or that over a term of years the trend of its graph is progressive, or mixed, or retrograde. The result is that where the yardstick of well-founded knowledge is lacking, none of us is forearmed against the prevalent urge of circumstances and of individual sentiment to crowd in on an already overcrowded market. Or, again, is it to be expected that in the absence of an adequate factual guide, the development of a multiple organisation, or the initiation of an advertising campaign can be as skilfully and as successfully promoted ?

Indeed, the value of more exact knowledge might be incalculable. This can be illustrated by a small but striking example taken from a recent publication of the

International Chamber of Commerce on Distributive Organisation in Europe and the United States. The case is of a hardware wholesaler who, after an intensive analysis followed by four years' application of the lessons that emerged, was able " to increase his net profits by 35 per cent. through reducing the number of his customers by 56 per cent., his sales' territory by 28 per cent., the variety of commodities sold by 30 per cent., and his sources of supply by 19 per cent."

Here is rationalisation in actual practice, and better than many a long-winded definition of its aims and scope. Moreover, the example is not untypical of what is waiting to be done at all stages. There has, for instance, recently been a statistical survey of eleven selected cities in the United States, and the material has been compiled into tables showing for each commodity where the main weight of the sales falls. The study was confined to " independent stores," but in summary it shows that 28 per cent. of their number had sales of less than $5000 a year, and accounted for only 2 per cent. of the total trade.

At the other end of the scale, 1 per cent. of their number accounted for 37 per cent. of the total trade. The following illuminating comment may be quoted :—

" To the sales departments of the manufacturing plants, tables such as these indicate the size of store best fitted to handle their products. Whereas the sales department of the manufacturing jeweller that fails to call on stores with sales of less than $5000 per year cuts itself off from 2 per cent. of the business, it saves the necessity for 30 per cent. of the total possible calls. The manufacturer who specialises in any of the many types of goods handled by department stores knows that if he is able to keep in contact with the best quarter of all the department stores, he will be dealing with those which handle 70 per cent. of the total department store business. It is information of this type which is gradually producing changes in the manufacturers' policy of sales and advertising. To the extent that the manufacturer can concentrate on the more important sales outlets, he saves sales expenses, reduces costs of distribution and exposes his business to less risk from credit." *

The general lie of the ground is now beginning to map itself out. Area surveys will have given us sociologically both a quantitative and a qualitative idea of the consumer's purse. Commodity surveys—at any rate so far as the really staple goods go—will have given us not only their effective demand in each area, but also to some extent their most appropriate types of distributive organisation. This will in turn enable us to postulate in the case of each commodity a reasonable optimum size for the shop unit, below which, on grounds of efficiency in operating costs, it will not be wise to drop. With this done it will then be possible to see how far, and in what respects, there is in actual practice a maladjustment, to which, of course, the special conditions of the area may be contributing. In other words, we shall be better able to locate and assess the extent and seriousness of the lag in desirable efficiency ; and at that point the healthy pressure which follows on enlightened knowledge will begin effectively to exert itself.

But ultimately it is difficult to avoid the deduction that knowledge, if it is to be put to adequate use, requires to be backed up by concerted action. The object

* *Note.*—Extract from a leaflet published by the Royal Bank of Canada, December, 1930.

will be to concentrate with a view to a lowering of costs, and the urgent need is that a common platform for such action should be found by all three parties—producer, distributor and consumer alike. This presupposes some form of representative organisation with authority to act for each party, and—still more important—a reasonable balance of responsible powers and forbearance between them.

At present there is little collective responsibility, and still less equilibrium, with the result that from time to time the consumer, in the person of Parliament, feels impelled to intervene with a piece of machinery that is intended to redress the balance. In this connection the general trend of legislation—actual and attempted—is significant, and the Agricultural Marketing Act of 1931 is a notable example to take.

Here it was obviously felt that a primary need was to secure better conditions for the producer by his enrolment into an approved organisation, and it was therefore laid down that an area-marketing scheme could be set on foot upon the application to the Minister by a substantially representative body of producers in that area. Providing that the scheme won approval—and admittedly there were many hurdles to overcome—the product would then become " regulated " and all producers " registered." Next, from among these producers a Board would be constituted, with very wide powers to develop production and to control marketing. It would act as the sole channel of purchase for the product, and in addition, as the arbiter of grading, packing, pricing and re-sale. As a result, the Board would be able to bestride a junction through which all consignments of the home product must pass ; and the interest of the Act may ultimately lie not so much in its clearly pre-scribed powers of compelling the producer for his own self-preservation to come into the organisation, as in its contingent reactions upon the present distributive struc-ture, about which nothing specific is said. Clearly the strategic initiative lies in the Board's hands. To take the case of milk, for instance, it could negotiate with the present distributive organisations and for that pur-pose would obviously be in a favoured position to effect a very keen settlement. But concurrently or alterna-tively it could, should it so desire, promote new dis-tributive agencies ; or else offer to the farmers, many of whom individually deliver their own milk, facilities for a greatly extended co-operative organisation.

Wherever therefore an agricultural product could be made largely a matter of home production, the Board would be bound to interest itself in efficient marketing equally with efficient production ; and in that event it could hardly avoid exercising pressure, with a view to the elimination of redundant units in distribution. Indeed, through its control of the key position, so much could be set in motion that a number of major problems which cannot even be tackled in the present ill-regulated state of things could be brought more easily within the realm of practical adjustment.

The most important point, however, is that here we have actually erected a new platform, which if properly used can be made to provide a different order of integra-tion between production and marketing. Further, there is implicit in its framework the idea of a collective trustee-ship for the successful organisation of certain products which are in daily and universal use.

Once that common platform is reached, hitherto un-observed but common interests begin to assert themselves and can become the predominant factor in a reshaping of problems. If, for example, we were to conceive, say, a new town of 20,000 to 30,000 inhabitants springing up in a hitherto rural district, few would gainsay the wisdom of a local authority co-operating with all concerned so as to make intelligent use of its powers in the planning of that town. Any zoning of the shopping area would be such an obviously sensible choice ; any conscious attempt to keep the number of shops progressively in step with the number of inhabitants would similarly be good ; for all parties to the arrangement would stand to benefit.

But we should not be right to conclude that this is merely a picture for the as yet unplanned town of to-morrow. The challenge which is for to-day is that we should set about liquidating the present position. Nor should it be overlooked that the temper of the people— witness the Consumers' Council Bill, the Food Council, the ordinary opinion of the man in the street—is levelled particularly against the shopkeeper who is near at hand, and whose inefficiencies are, therefore, more apparent than those of the unseen manufacturer. His case may have gone by default for the simple reason that although individually he has been concerned with selling everything " from an elephant to a pin," he has never in a corporate sense intelligently sold *himself*. To assist in a correction of that aspect of the matter, the earlier chapters of this

book have been directed, but at root there is a growing
feeling that the whole case no longer remains valid for the
nineteen-thirties. Nor does it. For we have allowed
circumstances to ride in the saddle in distribution just
as much as in production, and in production just as much
as in government and finance and other aspects of our
national life.

Our immediate concern, however, is with distribution's
redundancy, to which, as we have seen, there are many
contributory causes. Would it not be wise, therefore, to
encourage any helpful elements that may arise in the situation ? Let us, for instance, consider for a moment the
significance of the following table taken from a paper
read by Mr. W. Stanley Edgson, F.S.I., in December, 1929,
before the Auctioneers' and Estate Agents' Institute :

City.	Population.	Residential Hereditaments.	Retail Shops.	Houses per Shop.	Persons per Shop.	Shops with Rateable Value		
						Over £1000 p.a.	Between £100 and £1000 p.a.	Under £100 p.a.
Glasgow .	1,147,000	253,632	19,165	13·23	60·0	132	2,310	16,723
Birmingham	981,000	208,428	18,961	11·0	51·7	73	1,220	17,368
Liverpool .	866,000	181,387	21,800	8·32	39·7	—	—	—
Manchester	755,900	158,259	17,214	9·19	43·8	68	1,215	16,031

Let us further imagine that this information has been
supplemented by other statistics showing the thousand
or two grocers to each of these cities, the many hundreds
of shoe shops, butchers, drapers,—90 per cent. of them

confined within four walls * of a rateable value of less than
£100 per annum, and the lower end of them struggling
desperately under a miserable quota of trade and too
heavy a burden of stocks and expenditure.

A full picture of the poorer type of very small shop is
furnished by a private report that has been issued as the
result of a survey of the confectionery trade. This shows
first of all that something like 250,000 outlets in Great
Britain are selling cocoa or confectionery—generally, of
course, in conjunction with provisions or tobacco or other
commodities. The total itself is staggering enough, but
a classification of nearly 5000 of these shops, taken from
widely separated and differing districts, furnishes even
more striking data. The list is first of all divided into
five groups. In the upper half, classes 1 and 2 can be
graded as good to high-class shops ; class 3 is only
moderate. The description of the remaining two classes,
which it is estimated account for about half of the total
selling points for confectionery in the country, is given
verbatim :

" *Class* 4 are all shops of a distinctly inferior type ; a
very few are on main roads, the bulk of them being
general stores, beer stores, etc., on side roads. The
quality of goods stocked is not of the best, nor are they
always fresh. Many of these shops, if not positively

* The Inland Revenue Report (C.M.D. 3802) actually shows that
for the five years ending 1930 there were more than 50 per cent.
of the new lock-up shops (totalling 20,241 in all) with an annual
value for Schedule " A " purposes of under £40. Another interesting feature is that the total of new residential shops during the same
period reached 15,701, which is still not so very far below the
aggregate for lock-up shops.

objectionable in themselves, might be described as redundant.

" *Class* 5 consists exclusively of small dirty house shops in the slums, often doing a negligible trade in ' gob-stoppers,' liquorice bootlaces, etc., every one of which one could wish to see closed down."

The lesson is driven home by a brief description of the situation as it exists in one quarter of a depressed industrial town :—

" In certain parts the congestion of selling points is appalling. In two streets near the water front, for instance, each of which is about 300 yards long, there are no less than seventeen and sixteen selling points respectively. The population just here is very dense, it is true, the houses facing on to a series of courtyards branching off at right angles from the two streets ; none the less, three or four decent general shops in each street would amply serve their needs, and would provide a decent livelihood for half a dozen families instead of a mere pittance for over thirty. Neither of these streets are shopping streets in the ordinary sense. With the exception of two or three beer retailers, who also stock groceries and other household requirements, the shops are all house shops, and mostly of the poorest type."

With these pictures before us, let us now assume that, say, the Birmingham City Council has asked for powers under a Town Planning Act, first immediately to schedule the areas where shops should not extend further, and secondly to deal under perhaps a ten years' programme with existing shopping districts. Such a programme would again have zoning in view, the steady disappearance

of the uneconomic back-street shop, the curtailment of
the straggling outskirts.

The intricacies of the step might be considerable, and
one's first reaction to any scheme of legislative control
therefore unfavourable, but setting it against to-day's
depressing spread of retail outlets—and every town in
the country testifies to the truth of this description—
would it not be worth while at any rate to encourage the
courageous experiment ? For the manufacturer up and
down the country it would mean less dissipation of selling
effort and fewer losses from the dreary procession of
retail failures. For the remaining shopkeepers of that
town it should offer the possibility of far more efficient
and satisfactory trading. Accordingly, were they charged
with the duty of assisting as an organised body in the
liquidation of the position, it is not unreasonable to sup-
pose that it might prove to be worth their while even to
incur some small levy for this purpose, as has indeed
been voluntarily arranged under more difficult circumstances in one or two other industries. Alongside of this,
natural forces would be at work, such as the lapse of
leases and the disinclination of manufacturers or others
to extend indefinite support to scheduled areas. With the
nettle once seized, in fact, all factors could accelerate a
convergence of movement in the right direction. Nor,
apart from its scale, is it quite so revolutionary as it may
sound. The tenant shopkeeper has always had to face
the dislocation caused by the termination of his lease or
by rebuilding schemes ; and intermittent havoc has been
wrought by the fickle shift of trade further up or down
the street. Accordingly, any move to improve and con-

solidate conditions as a whole would tend to reduce hazards of this kind.

Such an experiment could, of course, be only one factor in tightening up the position, but it would add considerable definition to any internal efforts that industry itself might be putting forward to eliminate the present extremities of overlapping. In brief, here would be our common platform for an initial attack on the whole problem of reorganisation.

For it should be steadily kept in mind that measures of contraction can only be a means to an end—not an end in themselves. They are required to facilitate concentration and to hasten the selection of the best located channels for trading. With that movement definitely on foot we can the more certainly proceed with the positive work of bringing the whole scale and economy of production and distribution into line with the resources that science, and invention, and machine-power have placed at our disposal. There is a manifest need to drive new arterial roads through industry, to get rid of the narrow alleys and the blind corners. Distribution, with its first-hand knowledge of the public's needs, and its growing realisation of its capacity for massed purchasing power in staple commodities, might well set the pace for productive industry. Nor should we be true to our tradition if we shirked the issue. For, while it is the habit of the British people to eschew formulæ and to reject dogma, their very practical genius consists in an ability to work through new and changing forms.

GEORGE ALLEN & UNWIN LTD
London: 40 Museum Street, W.C.1
Cape Town: 73 St. George's Street
Sydney, N.S.W.: Wynyard Square
Auckland, N.Z.: 41 Albert Street
Toronto: 91 Wellington Street, West

For Product Safety Concerns and Information please contact our EU
representative GPSR@taylorandfrancis.com Taylor & Francis Verlag GmbH,
Kaufingerstraße 24, 80331 München, Germany

Printed and bound by CPI Group (UK) Ltd, Croydon, CR0 4YY
08/05/2025
01864525-0001